To: Sora
all the best!

3/18/14

SECOND STAGE ENTREPRENEURSHIP

Ten Proven Strategies for Driving
Aggressive Growth

DANIEL J. WEINFURTER

palgrave
macmillan

Dedication

To my Mom and Dad,

to Martha, Amy, and Andrea

and to my current and former colleagues

SECOND STAGE ENTREPRENEURSHIP
Copyright © Daniel J. Weinfurter, 2013.

All rights reserved.

First published in 2013 by
PALGRAVE MACMILLAN®
in the United States—a division of St. Martin's Press LLC,
175 Fifth Avenue, New York, NY 10010.

Where this book is distributed in the UK, Europe and the rest of the world,
this is by Palgrave Macmillan, a division of Macmillan Publishers Limited,
registered in England, company number 785998, of Houndmills,
Basingstoke, Hampshire RG21 6XS.

Palgrave Macmillan is the global academic imprint of the above companies
and has companies and representatives throughout the world.

Palgrave® and Macmillan® are registered trademarks in the United States, the
United Kingdom, Europe and other countries.

ISBN 978–1–137–30258–8

Library of Congress Cataloging-in-Publication Data

Weinfurter, Daniel J.
    Second stage entrepreneurship : ten proven strategies for driving
aggressive growth / Daniel J. Weinfurter.
        pages cm
    ISBN 978–1–137–30258–8 (alk. paper)
        1. Business planning. 2. Strategic planning. 3. Organizational change.
    I. Title.

HD30.28.W3755 2013
658.4′012—dc23   2013015912

A catalogue record of the book is available from the British Library.

Design by Newgen Knowledge Works (P) Ltd., Chennai, India.

First edition: October 2013

10 9 8 7 6 5 4 3 2 1

Printed in the United States of America.

CONTENTS

FIGURES

FOREWORD

THE MATURATION OF A START-UP into what Weinfurter refers to as a "second-stage" entrepreneurial business is a process fraught with challenges. If the start-up has demonstrated a product or service that is differentiated and value-added to its targeted customers, the multifaceted next phase involves growing the enterprise into a stable high-performing business. I have observed Dan lead such a maturation process, first as a director of and investor in his start-up Parson Group and then later, in a more limited incarnation, when Dan led an entrepreneurial effort within my large, established company, Caesars Entertainment.

Neither sheer smarts nor intuition are sufficient for any entrepreneur to move from starting a business to growing it into a significant enterprise. The activities, resources, competencies, and rewards are fundamentally different and require a much greater emphasis on process integrity and delegated control. While access to capital and the mechanisms through which capital is introduced into a new venture are critical and worthy of considerable debate, capital is the necessary condition for growth. The sufficient conditions include the key steps Weinfurter details, including governance, staffing, positioning, and, most interesting to me, selling.

First-year students at Harvard Business School, for example, learn a great deal about marketing. Indeed, marketing is properly seen as a critical function in nearly every successful business. However, generating revenue almost always requires one step beyond marketing: selling. Great sales and sales management, however, are not broadly taught in business schools and are not very well developed disciplines or practices. While good marketing conveys to the target a persuasive case for purchase along with critical information, such as price and availability, selling is a sustained, personal, and much more dynamic effort to convince a skeptical consumer that a product or service should be purchased. Take, for example, the case of philanthropy; a case I find particularly impressive when it is executed well. A development officer of a charity identifies you as a potential donor based on public and private information that ranges from recent wealth events to being a grateful patient or alumnus of an institution. The development officer begins a process with an investment of time and consideration that is not expected to bear fruit immediately, but is rather premised on the idea that sustained persuasion, gratitude, and high-touch contact will bring the donor to act.

Weinfurter grew up in sales at GE and knows the process better than anyone I have met. Dan's own entrepreneurial ventures have been built largely around excellence in sales. His book teaches us how to build an organization of sales people and sales management that can consistently advance the position of our products and services by hiring, training, measuring, and rewarding the right talent to execute a well-articulated strategy for sales. In so doing, the sales function becomes a key part of the firm's differentiation rather than a necessary or costly evil. His process includes matching the sales executive to the target, monitoring and refining activity and pitch, relentlessly managing performance, and constantly refilling and refining the sales team to enhance effectiveness.

Several years ago, I observed that my own company was very good at marketing but not nearly so adept at selling. We did not hire, train, or manage for sales proficiency and lacked the systems to do so. Dan joined us as a consultant and quickly established the hiring, sales management, and sales training systems that have blossomed into a meaningful source of revenue generation for the company.

If you have made the considerable step forward to establish a business and have demonstrated that it can meet a differentiated need in the marketplace, you owe it to yourself and your investors to develop the organizational capacity to carefully build a plan to mature the start-up into a robust growth enterprise. Weinfurter has a rigorous, straightforward method for doing so that can and should be executed by entrepreneurs who are determined to overcome the frequent pitfalls that accompany the transition from start-up to second stage. While we all appreciate the differences and nuances of our own businesses, there are some fundamental principles that transcend these distinctions. Dan presents these fundamental principles and then concludes with his own reflections on shaping the customer experience, developing your culture, and maturing as an effective leader. I have learned a great deal from watching Dan hone the ideas you will find in his book, and I am confident you will too.

GARY LOVEMAN
Chairman and CEO of
Caesar's Entertainment

ACKNOWLEDGMENTS

THIS BOOK HAS BEEN A WORK in process for a number of years. After receiving encouragement from a few people who I worked with over the years and know well, I made the commitment to actually dedicate my efforts to completing this book beginning in late 2011. I owe many people my thanks and gratitude for making this book possible.

First on this list are my parents, Betty and Joe Weinfurter. I am one of eight children, all of us born and raised in Wauwatosa, Wisconsin, a middle-class suburb of Milwaukee. I have many things to thank my parents for, certainly far too many to list here. However, a few things they instilled in me stand out: the value of working hard, but not so hard that there is no time for fun along the way, staying connected to friends and family despite the passage of time and the constraints of geography, and a lifelong passion for learning. My parents, currently 90 and 91, just celebrated their sixty-fourth anniversary. They still each read nearly an entire book every day, live completely on their own, and both still drive. I hope to age as gracefully as they have, and aspire to be as good a role model to my kids as they have been to me.

Since I started my career at GE right out of Marquette University, I have had the good fortune to be part of a number of great organizations and work with many supremely talented and dedicated professionals. In addition, there are perhaps a dozen or so very special and talented individuals that I worked with in more than one company, in some cases going all the way back to the early days in my career when I was at GE. The success that has sometimes been attributed to me should really be shared by all of the individuals at the various organizations who made this success possible. Business is after all a supreme team sport.

There are many others who have contributed to this book in ways they perhaps don't realize. The companies I have been involved with have all had investors, including both individuals and institutional private equity firms. Having an individual part with his or her hard-earned cash for what is just an idea takes real courage, and the partners at private equity firms likewise take on risk with every new investment. I will always be indebted to the investors of both Parson Group and Capital H Group. Their willingness to take a chance on an entrepreneur with an idea and a plan made those companies possible. The growth of these companies was helped in no small part by a number of advisors and friends along the journey, including commercial banks, insurance and real estate brokers, investment bankers, lawyers, other vendors, and consultants. Finally, in all cases, we were fortunate to have a large number of fantastic clients who also found the courage to take a chance with a new, unbranded service provider. For some reason, these people, who in most cases worked for large organizations, were willing to assume the career risk that comes from breaking away from conventional behavior (and also ignoring the purchasing department's directives to stick with established vendors), and taking a chance with a new firm with a limited track record but a perhaps a different value proposition and approach from what they had previously heard from their current providers. Without clients or customers, even brilliant plans or clever ideas do not matter very much.

For a first-time writer, the lack of knowledge on the steps necessary to write and publish a book might appear overwhelming. I was fortunate enough to be initially guided through this process by Melissa Giovagnoli Wilson, who provided advice on how to navigate through this maze from the beginning, starting with the basics—the proper way to write a book proposal. Melissa introduced me to John Willig, who subsequently became my agent, and John provided both sage guidance and support as well as the occasional (and needed) tough love as the proposal, title, and focus of the book was reshaped through the process to meet what was needed in the market. Paul Dinas and Rusty Fisher provided valuable assistance in writing, editing, and reorganizing the book's content as we worked through the manuscript drafting process. Laurie Harting, executive editor at Palgrave Macmillan, was a joy to work with. I greatly appreciate her support of this project and her willingness to take on the risk to work with a first-time author. She has demonstrated a passion for entrepreneurs and what they try to make possible.

My thanks go out to the CEOs of the companies profiled as case studies as well as the others who agreed to be interviewed for this book. It is their unique stories that hopefully make some of the main points in the book come to life. As most would acknowledge, agreeing to talk to a writer is not for the faint of heart, as you never really know what will ultimately be written and attributed to you. Hopefully, I have faithfully and accurately rendered all of those conversations into the text of this book. I appreciate all of you taking time to talk to me about your businesses, your successes, as well as the things you would do differently if given the chance.

For me, in addition to having the privilege of working with great people throughout my business career, I had the added benefit of having the complete support of my wife and family, which has proven to be extraordinarily helpful on so many levels. Starting multiple companies from scratch that become international in scale over time by necessity results in many days on the road and many evenings and weekends tied up in activities related to the business. Writing a book also involves significant time and effort. Without support at home, none of this would have been possible. I am most grateful for their love and support.

DAN WEINFURTER

Chicago, IL

August, 2013

INTRODUCTION

REAL LEARNING MOMENTS COME OUT OF challenging and difficult situations and experiences. Founding a business is certainly one that belongs in the challenging category. It takes vision, determination, market timing, and capital resources to make it a success. Starting a business and making it grow beyond the initial start-up has been a lifelong passion for me. Over the years, my partners and I have been fortunate to make that dream a reality more than once.

My approach has been to be focused on growth from the very beginning, always looking ahead to the next phase in the development of the business. However, most entrepreneurs operate with a different model, one that has two distinct phases. It begins with a vision about a business that offers something new or fills a market need. In the start-up phase the founder is focused primarily on proof of concept, essentially getting to a point where there is a viable product, service, or functional geographic location.

Once the business is established and generating steady revenue and predictable profits, the founder makes a decision to move the business to the next stage and become a second-stage entrepreneur. Second-stage entrepreneurs think bigger and have a passion to serve more customers by expanding their business. This takes planning, drive, creativity, new capital, and most of all, a willingness to change the organization to meet new goals.

My career in business started in one of the biggest companies of all, General Electric Company. I spent eight years at GE, all in sales, sales support, and sales management. Much of my view of the business world was formed during my time there. Armed with the skills I'd learned, and after a couple of other stops along the way, I decided to start my own business from scratch. That company was called Parson Group. It was started from the very beginning with the goal of rapid growth and capitalized with the help of an investor group. The business plan contained the principal strategies I will talk about in this book that drive rapid growth from the start-up phase into the second stage of growth and beyond.

The path to second-stage growth in business is not straight or predictable. Many of the assumptions we make as part of our plan often turn out to be insufficient or just flat-out wrong. A strategy for one kind of business may not work for another kind of business. A plan that works well in one part of the country does not guarantee success in another—or in a different country. A tactic that worked well in 1995 may no longer work in 2013. Markets shift and competitors proliferate; the economy rises and falls. As the saying goes, change is the only constant. The successful second-stage entrepreneur has to remain open and responsive to unanticipated changes to achieve sustained growth.

What does it mean to bring your company to second-stage growth? According to research assembled by the Edward Lowe Foundation in 2012, a second-stage growth company is a business that has progressed past its start-up phase but has not achieved its full potential.[1] The typical size of a second-stage growth company is between ten and one hundred employees, with revenues between one million and fifty million dollars. While this group comprises upward of 10 percent of all American businesses, it is responsible for over 36 percent of total employment and 38 percent of all sales. These numbers are impressive and indicate that a substantial segment of the small business community is successful at attaining additional growth.

While it is illuminating to learn these statistics regarding second stage growth companies, they can be limiting. Second-stage entrepreneurship is more of a process of transforming the way one thinks about one's company. Rather than describe it in terms of size and revenue, I believe that in most cases, the transition is best described as beginning when the founder feels confident that the start-up is solidly successful and continues until the founder chooses to exit. Second-stage growth is a launching pad for continued growth.

This book offers ten proven strategies that apply to any successful start-up seeking to achieve this all-important goal. I've chosen a handful of second-stage companies and illustrate how they employed one or more of these strategies to achieve success. Whether your company is based on a business-to-business model (B2B) or a business-to-consumer model (B2C), the basic goal is the same: expand the business and increase profitability. While there are different challenges inherent in each of these models, they share the fundamental tools for growth: creativity, the right staff, unique corporate culture, proactive management practices, smart governance, strong leadership, and new capitalization. In my experience, these precepts are universal and will help propel any business forward.

Is it easy? No. Does one solution fit every kind of business? Certainly not. As David Lee, the prominent Silicon Valley venture capitalist said when speaking about the current business climate, "It has never been easier to start a company and never harder to build one."[2]

But with savvy knowledge of your business and of the industry and market in which you operate, adherence to a solid business plan, and the determination and grit to make it happen, you can become a successful second-stage entrepreneur.

Chapter 1

GROW OR DIE

STARTING A COMPANY IS HARD WORK. Every entrepreneur can attest to that fact. Assembling the capital, creating systems, hiring staff, finding customers, keeping the momentum going to make it a success—these tasks are all-consuming. It is no wonder that owners become so invested in their start-ups that when it comes time to take the business to the second stage of development, they often hesitate, or even stall. The business is running well and making a profit. The staff is working at capacity and content. The temptation is to rely on the current systems, products, and talent to take the company to the next level.

However, this is not a viable strategy for sustained growth. In order to reach second-stage development, much of what made your start-up a success will need to change. This is difficult, as there will be times when the entrepreneur does not know what he or she does not know. This is untraveled territory. Second-stage entrepreneurship involves the reevaluation of the entire organization, including your relationship with it. Once you've made the decision to expand, there's no looking back. It has got to be: grow or die.

TIMING IS EVERYTHING

The decision to grow the company is not a simple one. Certainly, a big question relates to timing. Is now the time to grow? If not now, when? The answer to this question has two parts. First, there is the personal part of the decision. Are you as the founder really ready to press ahead? Do you possess the capability, motivation, and capacity to take the company to the next stage? After all, the decision to drive toward second-stage growth involves significant risk of failure, possibly the loss of everything you've worked so hard to build. It's not only a business decision; it is personal as well.

Part two of the question relates to the external business environment. Is the market for your products or services healthy and growing quickly enough for you to grow with it? What's the state of the general economy? Can customers keep current with their commitments? How will current fluctuations in interest rates and inflation affect your bottom line? Is sufficient capital available to fund growth? Are changes in technology moving more quickly than you are? How aggressive are your competitors? Answers to these and dozens of other timing issues need to inform your decision on when to push the button on your strategy for growth. We have all learned over the years that timing, in fact, does matter. The following example of a successful health care services firm shows why timing is such a key factor in the decision to initiate second-stage growth.

MIDWEST HEALTH CARE SERVICES FIRM

Consider the situation facing a Midwest-based start-up health care services firm that is owned equally by its two founding entrepreneurs. The mission of this firm is to transform health care by empowering individual employees to take control of their own health. It claims that if companies implement its suggested approach, they can reduce their overall health care expenses by more than 30 percent and still deliver a much higher level of health care and thus better overall health for their employees. There is a huge market opportunity for the services this company provides, and its initial locations have performed well from a financial perspective and have been very successful in the fulfillment of the company mission—for the employees and for the corporate sponsors. It would seem obvious that the entrepreneurs need to expand quickly to take advantage of their market opportunity. But this organization currently lacks both the financial resources and the human capital to execute a second-stage growth plan. It needs to take on outside capital to fund the necessary investments for more rapid growth.

However, the two owners have a different view on taking on external capital. One fears the loss of control that comes from outside investors. The other is deeply concerned that if they don't execute a growth plan, they will miss the market opportunity with potentially disastrous results as their competitors are well funded and aggressive. The market is moving quickly. While the external factors indicate the time is right to grow, one partner is not ready to take the leap.

BEING A SECOND-STAGE ENTREPRENEUR

No one becomes a second-stage entrepreneur overnight. It is a process in which you have to change your mind-set from being a scrappy start-up entrepreneur, involved in every aspect of your business, calling all the shots, each and every day, doing whatever it takes to make your company succeed. And your efforts have paid off. The business is finally taking off. Customers are pouring in. Everything is coming together. You're even making money.

Then it dawns on you. Your start-up is a success. And while you are growing, you know your business could be so much more: bigger, better, and grabbing more market share with new products and services. It's time to make the move, to make plans to bring it to the next stage. As the plan becomes a reality, suddenly you can no longer keep abreast of every critical event and decision that occur, or need to occur, every minute of every day. There is more to do than you can physically accomplish on your own. It's time to realize that you need a plan for growth and, more important, some outside help.

Letting go is one of hardest lessons any founder has to learn about second-stage entrepreneurship. In the beginning, owners are involved in every decision concerning their businesses—from what color to paint the front office to how to structure the sales team. The second-stage entrepreneur has to focus on the bigger picture and not obsess over all the small stuff. This is not to say that certain details do not matter. After all, it was your vision and drive that got the business going. Now you must learn the importance of leveraging your unique skills to make the next leap. Organizational process, discipline, and a sufficiently well articulated and widely understood vision for the future become critical to lead the company into second-stage success. Delegating responsibilities to the right management team and leading the charge must be your new role.

THE IMPORTANCE OF A NEW BUSINESS PLAN

Things will move quickly once you make the commitment to grow your company. But how quickly do you want to grow? The timetable you make will shape the next step in the process: your new business plan. It shows both what *can* be done, but equally important, it also shows what *must* be done for the business to deliver the planned results on schedule.

For instance, the decisions on the capital strategy and on the growth strategy are highly intertwined. Typically, growth comes from a series of individual investments that, when executed correctly, tend to pay off with a resulting increase in sales and profits. Decisions can be as straightforward as how many salespeople to add and when to add them (assuming a business model that grows through a professional selling organization) or as complicated as creating a new product line with all of the research, development, engineering, manufacturing, packaging, pricing, marketing, and selling efforts this will involve. Each step takes time.

These types of decisions, when combined with staffing concerns, new systems and support, additional channels of distribution, facility expansion, and dozens of other considerations, make the business planning exercise one of the most challenging and complicated steps toward second-stage growth.

CHANGING YOUR OPERATING STRATEGY

When the initial version of the basic business plan is done, the real work begins. Commitment to growth means commitment to changing business as usual. Personnel changes are among the first consider-ations and often the hardest. Can the existing managers and employ-ees propel the company to new growth? If new people are needed, will they be in addition to or replacements of the current staff? How much restructuring needs to occur to create effective new teams?

A classic example of this kind of basic personnel change is the structure of an internal finance and accounting department. Start-ups rarely have multilayered financial departments. Typically, there's a bookkeeper, an accounts receivable person, an accounts payable per-son, and a payroll person. Sometimes one person wears all of these hats. However, if a company plans to grow its organization and rev-enue significantly, this structure won't work. A second-stage company will certainly require an accounting manager to oversee the balance sheet and financial reporting. Soon, a controller will be necessary, and at some point in the second stage, a CFO is likely to be necessary. And it is highly unlikely that the person who is currently wearing the many hats to keep your accounting operation running smoothly will also be the best fit for the CFO role. These are fundamentally different roles, requiring very different levels of skill, education, and experience. Preparing for second-stage growth will have you asking this same question for different roles throughout your organization. And, if you are honest, you will likely come to the conclusion that there are cer-tain individuals that for some reason don't have the necessary horse-power to go to the next level. This is a painful process that results in the loss of some of the key people who helped get you to your current position. However, making these decisions in a thoughtful fashion is a necessary process for driving future growth. How this new level of management will impact existing staff is a big consideration as well.

BUST TO BOOM

When you talk with the owners of Founders Brewing Co., Mike Stevens and Dave Engbers, they will be the first to tell you that they struggled to keep the doors of their fledgling microbrewery open. Ten years earlier, they had quit their full time jobs and decided to pursue their passion for beer by starting their own brewing business, commencing in typical beer industry fashion as a brew pub. After an extended start-up period, they experimented with different mixtures and created a line of good but not particularly remarkable lagers. Located in downtown Grand Rapids, Michigan, Founders Brewing Co. had a solid local reputation, but it could not draw a critical mass.[1] Debts mounted; sales growth came slowly. Dave and Mike had to do something or see their dream disappear. They had to grow or die.

In 2007, perhaps out of desperation, they decided to commit to a new strategy. Rather than compete with others for a piece of the lager market, they decided to use their expertise to create a line of totally new, premium-priced products that were more aromatic and had bigger, bolder tastes, such as Founders Brewing Breakfast Stout.[2] This unusual beer contains coffee, chocolate, and oatmeal. It has an alcohol content of over 8 percent. With the help of some new capital, they changed the packaging and expanded their line to include unique beers with catchy names such as Double Trouble, All Day Pale Ale, Devil Dancer, Curmudgeon Stout, Bad Habit, and Dirty Bastard.

This strategy was rewarded when they were invited to attend the invitation-only, Extreme Beer Fest in Boston, an annual event put on by *BeerAdvocate*, one of the most respected print and online publications of the microbrewery industry. This event was *the* defining moment for Founders Brewing. They had lines out the door for the entire event. The editors of *BeerAdvocate* came to talk to them to try to understand the tremendous buzz about this "upstart brewery."

When the Founder's team drove back to Grand Rapids from Boston in Dave Engbers father's Mercury Sable station wagon, the founders recommitted themselves to a last-ditch effort to take the company to the next level. The rest is history. It took Founders ten years to get to an annual production of 10,000 barrels of beer, a serious milestone for the company and well beyond the industry breakeven point of 3,000 to 6,000 barrels, according to Lueders Consulting, an industry expert.[3] In the years immediately after the relaunch, annual production volume grew as follows: 17,000 barrels, 28,000 barrels, 43,000 barrels, 71,000 barrels, and now it tops 135,000 barrels. With a new production facility currently under construction, production capacity will grow to over 350,000 barrels.

SHIFTGIG

The technology industry today operates by a set of rules different from those that govern other second-stage entrepreneurs. Like many who have started a business, entrepreneurs in this industry initially focus on building a minimum viable product and then learning the product's strengths and weaknesses, the market it serves, and trying to build some initial user experience. Unlike the rest of the world, they don't worry about revenue. Rather, in this stage, they focus on the number of users of their software and user feedback. This stage is often financed by the founders in an effort to keep full control of the company to maximize their opportunity for value creation. But time is compressed in the world of technology, and the second stage often comes after a number of months, not a number of years.

Shiftgig was started in late 2011 by Eddie Lou. Eddie's background is unique in that he started in the business world first as an entrepreneur, then became a venture capitalist, and then left that world to start Shiftgig together with two cofounders. The idea behind Shiftgig is to connect individuals who have experience in the hospitality industry as bartenders, waiters, and cooks with establishments that are looking to hire individuals with these skills. Think of Shiftgig as a cross between a LinkedIn platform focused on the hospitality industry and aspects of Facebook. Individuals can input their skills and experience on the Shiftgig platform much as they would do it on LinkedIn, but they can also add other elements, such as video, additional photos, and their "social score" as demonstrated by showing the number of Facebook friends and Twitter followers. This provides a very efficient way for employers to find exactly the kind of person who will fit into their bar or restaurant.

During the first six months of Shiftgig's existence, the emphasis was on building the product and getting an initial user base, first in Chicago and soon thereafter in New York and Los Angeles, all cities with large numbers of bars and restaurants. But even while the product was in its initial launch phase, Eddie was hard at work developing the plan for a national rollout coupled with determining the optimal approach to set up a Series A round of funding to support this growth plan. In less than a year after the company's founding, Shiftgig closed on a $3 million round intended to fund the next stage of the company's growth.

GROW OR DIE

Grow or die. This is quite a polarizing statement and, of course, if taken literally, some might take issue with it. Certainly there are many companies that either do not grow at all or grow very slowly. Many of these are great businesses that have been around for years, generate a great deal of cash, and provide a very nice lifestyle for their owners. I have met the CEOs of dozens of companies that are under $10 million in annual revenue, yet their businesses produce hundreds of thousands of dollars or even millions in profit each year, most of which is taken as a distribution by the owner. In many ways, it is hard to argue against this approach. It can and often does fund a very nice lifestyle.

However, this approach has never been for me, and likely it is also not for the readers of this book. To have the desire to continuously and rapidly grow a business is very rewarding, and in many ways, at least in my view of the world, it is the only approach that will work over an extended period of time.

Let me explain why. In a subsequent chapter of this book, I will explain that in the long run, talent is the only true sustainable competitive advantage. If you want to grow and prosper over time, you *have* to figure out how to get very talented people into the key roles in your company—and keep them there. This tenet, I believe, is self-evident.

But people of real talent, ones with considerable capability, potential, and ambition are also looking for growth opportunities, both personally and professionally. Most truly talented people will only stay in a role for so long unless they are continuously challenged, and along with this environment of challenge they want opportunities to engage in continuous learning and career advancement.

It works the same way in sports, for instance. After all, does a really good tennis player want to play against someone he or she can easily beat? Or if you were a chess player, would you prefer someone as an opponent who is not very astute and you can easily beat? Or would you prefer to play against someone who is better, even if this means you are unlikely to win? Competitive people value real competition just as talented people demand to be challenged so they can learn and they can grow. Yes, compensation also matters, but it will likely be insufficient on its own to keep your very best employees on board.

So, in order to provide opportunities for your most talented people to grow into roles and situations of increasing complexity, it is necessary for the entire enterprise to also grow. The growth of the business creates a need for someone to step up, and with talented individuals you have a cadre of folks to choose from who can stretch into these new roles and bring with them their unique capability, experience, and drive. This works far better than trying to convince the same person to do essentially the same job for the next two years.

The real beauty of this entire cycle is that it is self-reinforcing. Really talented people tend to create great outcomes for customers and clients, whether by the product they design or make or by the service they deliver. The quality in the product or service delivery results in significant improvements in the value as perceived by these customers and also in their overall level of satisfaction. Improvements in value received and overall satisfaction levels result in higher levels of growth for the business, and this growth in turn results in yet more opportunities for personal and professional growth for the employees. Yes, everyone is happy when you can pull this off. Of course, there is a potential downside to this strategy: if you have built your team by selling the growth story and for whatever reason you can't pull this off or growth slows, you may be challenged to keep your best people as they will seek out alternative situations that can deliver a more compelling set of growth opportunities.

PARTING WORDS

Making the decision to grow aggressively presents serious risks to any business, emotionally and financially. Make sure that the decision is based on solid business planning. Growth for growth's sake is not a sustainable strategy. A successful start-up can remain just that if market conditions don't warrant investment in serious growth.

Second-stage entrepreneurship takes a commitment to a new vision for the future and the solid plan to accomplish it. It will mean fundamental changes to a company and the founder's relationship with it. New money, new decision makers, new products, new systems will be necessary to scale up the business. With the total commitment of the founder and his or her team plus a well-reasoned business plan, executed under the right market conditions, your company can achieve successful growth. And when you do this, well, few things in life are more rewarding.

Chapter 2

NEW CAPITAL SOURCES

PERHAPS NO TOPIC DRAWS SUCH heated controversy among entrepreneurs as how to finance second-stage growth. Unless the start-up is so successful that it has accumulated a substantial war chest of cash to fund the push to the next level, new capital will be needed. There are a variety of sources for new capital, each of them with its own set of issues concerning accountability, control, and profitability for the second-stage entrepreneur. Needless to say, the typical founder prefers the option with the least strings attached, but given the size of the funding required, this may not be feasible.

YOUR BUSINESS AND NEW CAPITAL

As with many fundamental business decisions, the decision about how much new capital is required and on what timetable depends on your business plan for second-stage growth. In order to thoroughly evaluate your need for new capital, the business plan needs to address the following questions:

1. What is your strategy for growth?
2. What is the current debt exposure?
3. What is projected revenue before recapitalization or new capital coming into the business?
4. What is the projected total cost of the investments that underlie the growth strategy?
5. What is the time line necessary for the capital infusion?

This information is critical for you to make a decision about your growth capital needs. In addition, it will also help you to formulate a strategy about your approach for the additional funding you need. Potential investors will also need to know all or most of this information before committing funds.

BANKS AND LENDING INSTITUTIONS

The traditional source of funding is a bank or some other financial institution that offers debt or mezzanine financing. In today's economy, lending institutions are cautious about loans to companies that are not yet well established. The common wisdom when dealing with banks is that until you get to a threshold level of profit/EBITDA of $5 million, debt financing will require collateralization by the assets of the business and in many instances a personal guarantee as well. These requirements limit your borrowing capability significantly. In addition to the strict requirements, it can take months for a loan application to make its way to through the many layers of approval in the present post-meltdown banking environment. For second-stage business development, timing is critical. Unless you can build this approval time into your business plan, it is time you can't afford.

FRIENDS AND FAMILY

A large number of new businesses start out with money from personal connections. An entrepreneur has an idea and solicits money from a group of personal and family contacts. The benefits of this source are obvious. The lenders are personally invested in seeing you and your business succeed, and therefore their attitude regarding the loan does not come with the usual skepticism, caveats, and high interest rates of a lending institution. Friends and family can be quite helpful in driving business to the venture and offering to pitch in to help in a variety of ways. Access to the funds is faster and involves far less red tape—an important factor when you are in a growth mode.

The primary drawbacks of relying on personal connections for financing are significant, however. Unless you move in millionaire circles, it is difficult to raise meaningful amounts of capital from family and friends. In order to reach your capitalization goal from this source, you may need to piece together a hodgepodge of small amounts from a large number of contacts, which can get complicated and difficult to keep track of.

Growing a company is a process fraught with all kinds of unforeseen challenges and pitfalls. There is no guarantee of success and a high likelihood of failure. According to a recent New York University Working Paper, financing from friends and family often leads to suboptimal results.[1] For many entrepreneurs, the aversion to taking chances significantly increases because of fear to put the capital from personal contacts at risk. You are committed to your business and willing to take certain calculated risks to make it a second-stage success. However, involving friends and family can hold you back from some of the more aggressive plans for future growth you might otherwise execute, sometimes to the detriment of the business.

HIGH-NET-WORTH PRIVATE INVESTORS

High-net-worth private investors differ from friends and family in that they are professional businesspeople who invest for profit. Often referred to as angel investors, they are open to compelling investment opportunities and are less risk-averse than traditional lenders. They may or may not be officially part of a firm, but they apply many of the same rigorous standards to any potential investment partner.

Purely from the perspective of numbers, high-net-worth investors occupy a large and growing segment of the financing market for small businesses. According to Startupnation.com, over 250,000 high-net-worth private investors fund over 30,000 small companies at all levels of development each year.[2] This includes start-ups as well as second-stage companies. In 2012, about 40 percent of the total dollars invested by high-net-worth investors went to seed financing, with the balance going to fund subsequent stages of growth.

If you do not have a history of entrepreneurial or significant corporate success and your business is still at an early stage, the full potential of the business model might appear unproven to institutional lenders. But because of the less rigid and often subjective criteria of high-net-worth investors, the latter are a great source of financing for new growth. They base their decisions on their experience with small business and bring a great deal of expertise to the table.

High-net-worth private investors have a particular interest in funding young companies poised for second-stage success. In many cases, these investors made their fortunes as entrepreneurs who built their own businesses and then cashed out at a considerable profit. They can identify with the second-stage entrepreneur. Their motivation to fund small companies moving into second-stage growth usually involves more than return on investment. They often are committed to giving back to the small business community by staying intellectually engaged by investing in promising ideas and talented management teams.

This dynamic has become a self-reinforcing cycle, especially in certain parts of the country where there has been a great deal of entrepreneurial success such as Boston, Chicago, Austin, New York, and the San Francisco Bay area. While there are outlier examples of high-net-worth investors lending millions to a promising new company, the investment usually ranges between $100,000 and $1 million.

Many of these high-net-worth investors form groups to pool their investment dollars, share research, expertise across industries, and financial risk. These groups are not difficult to find. Many are industry-specific and will maintain a high profile within that community. Their application requirements and investment criteria, such as the range of investment capital available and minimum revenue and profitability targets, are available on their web sites. There are also firms that specialize in steering second-stage entrepreneurs to these groups, but there is a meaningful fee for these services.

By doing some basic research and networking with other business professionals knowledgeable about your industry, you can easily connect with these groups directly. They are not trying to keep their existence a secret. On the contrary, they are always looking for new and exciting opportunities. Depending on the success of your start-up and the strength of your business growth plan, you should be able to find an individual or group open to hearing your presentation. After your initial pitch, these groups can move quickly if they are interested.

As is the case with most outside capital sources, the principal drawback of high-net-worth investors involves cost and control. The investors will likely demand a percentage of your company in exchange for their investment, generally a pro-rata percentage of the company based on funded investment capital compared to the enterprise value of the company. In most cases, they require a great deal of oversight as well. It is not uncommon for one or more of these investors to require a seat on the board of your company. As board members, they will have considerable input into all decisions regarding your company.

If you accept new capital from these investors, it is critical to set the rules of engagement from the beginning. For example, the rules can call for investor membership on the board in either a voting or non-voting capacity. There is a fair amount of variability between various angel investors on the format, level of detail, and frequency of communication to the investor group regarding operational and financial decisions; understand the ground rules up front so you understand how much time you will be spending with your investor group. While high-net-worth investors can be great partners and share their experience and industry insights concerning your second-stage growth strategies, you need to be able to agree on and live with the level of their involvement in your business before taking their money.

VENTURE CAPITALISTS

Venture capitalists specialize in new unproven companies that offer high potential but also high risk. They can be individuals, groups, or established firms. In 2012, according to the National Venture Capital

Association, the institutional venture capital industry invested over $26 billion in over 4,000 companies, with about 25 percent of those firms receiving financing for the first time.[3] Venture capitalists have a higher risk-to-success ratio as well. They experience a 40 percent failure rate, with only 20 percent hitting their ROI targets. The failure rate of venture-backed companies, while still high, is quite a bit better than the commonly held view that over 75 percent of all new start-ups fail.

Venture capitalists have provided funding for most of the companies we have come to associate with big-time entrepreneurial success. In addition to all the examples of start-ups that have become common household names (Facebook, Google, Zip Cars, Zappos, CDW Computers, Twitter, etc.), there are literally thousands of examples of companies that you may or may not have heard of that have moved from start-up to the second stage and then well beyond with venture capital investment funding their growth.

PRIVATE EQUITY FIRMS

Venture capitalists and private equity firms are often referred to as though they were the same thing. However, they are actually different types of investors. As we've seen, venture capitalists typically invest in relatively high-risk new companies they deem to have high potential. They can be individuals or groups. In exchange for their investment, they exact a hefty percentage of the ownership of your firm and often require some significant oversight of the company.

Private equity firms, on the other hand, are organized primarily as investment businesses. They target existing businesses that need capital or financial assistance to grow, or in many cases they believe that a number of similar businesses can be combined to create a more efficient and much more valuable larger company, often referred to as build-ups or roll-ups. Private equity investors recognize that companies of a certain size generally trade for a higher multiple of earnings than smaller companies in the same industry. In exchange for substantial capital, they typically will seek to acquire majority control of the business in question. Generally, the original owner and the current management team cede ultimate decision-making power to the private equity partner although in practice, as operators, the management team still has a fair amount of day-to-day control. Private equity investment is considered by some as a last resort source of capital to save the company or as exit strategy for the owner. Many others view private equity investment as a very effective strategy for an entrepreneur who needs a deep-pocketed financial partner to fund a high-growth company where significant capital will be required to execute the growth plan.

Private equity offers access to the largest pool of investment capital of any group. According to a 2012 Bain & Company report, over $3 trillion of capital is on the books of institutional private equity firms, with over a third of this still as dry powder.[4] While they have the deepest pockets, they also seek the most aggressive level of involvement and control of the companies in which they invest.

The investments of private equity firms cover literally every industry and include what are now emerging or midsize companies, such as True Partners Consulting, LA Fitness, Yankee Candle, Miller-Heiman, E-Loan, CHI Overhead Door, and Sunrise Senior Living. Private equity firms also have provided a significant amount of later stage capital that was needed for nearly all the companies we mentioned earlier that have gone from start-up to significant size over the past twenty years.[5] To grow rapidly requires substantial capital.

While there is a great deal of money available from both venture capitalists and private equity firms and they tend to move faster than traditional lenders, they are not especially creative when it comes to their investment guidelines. In other words, you will need to fit into their model, and they tend not to be willing to customize their criteria for investing. Each firm has its own rules about the size of its investments, the industries it favors, minimum revenue and EBITDA requirements, and acceptable operating models.

For example, some firms only like recurring revenue models that are highly resistant to recessions. Others invest exclusively in specific industries, such as technology or health care. Some develop investment themes, such as "infrastructure" or "big data." It is a high-stakes world that does not suffer sloppiness lightly. You have to do your homework, know your options, and be prepared to trade off some or most of your control for enough capital to grow.

If this is your first time in the realm of seeking high-level investment capital, expect the hurdles to be high. Most of these professional investors want to back entrepreneurs who have already had considerable success in a very similar venture. This condition makes it particularly difficult for you as second-stage entrepreneur unless your start-up has been extremely profitable, has grown rapidly already, or is in a very hot market area the investors want to enter or expand into. They will also want you to coinvest personally as a precondition for their own investment. If you don't have the ability to write a check in the high six figures, working with these professional investors may be difficult.

Expect a high level of scrutiny for everything you do. Detailed monthly operational calls and/or meetings as well as formal quarterly board meetings are standard practice. Preparation for these meetings is time-consuming, and you will spend at least two days a month preparing for and engaging in conversations with your private equity or venture capital investor.

In the case of both venture capital and private equity investors, perhaps the most difficult aspect for you as entrepreneur remains the loss of control over the business you have built. This loss of control is often a deal breaker for many entrepreneurs. For others it is a completely fair trade-off for obtaining the necessary capital resources to fund rapid growth. While it is possible to maintain significant control, this can be complicated. Typically, you will need a business that already has some considerable scale and is looking for growth capital that in aggregate is less than 50 percent of the current valuation of your business.

However, even in cases where the founder retains significant control, there are likely to be provisions in the investment agreement that trigger the loss of control if certain financial metrics are not met. Predicting financial outcomes with some certainty over an extended time period is not an easy task, and what appears to be a remote possibility can become reality if market or economic conditions change.

Just before the full depth of the financial meltdown became evident in late 2008, my firm was struggling like many others at that time. Before the crash, we had nearly 50 percent of our revenue coming from global financial services firms. In the course of the second half of 2007, this revenue stream eroded significantly.

On Christmas Eve that year, I took a call from my private equity partner. He had seen all the reports and knew the economic storm clouds were gathering although we did not know at the time how bad it would ultimately be. The conversation was short and to the point. "Dan, I just called to remind you that the only thing that matters to me and to my partners, the only thing, is financial results," he said. "Merry Christmas, by the way." Then he hung up. Seriously, this was the conversation. It was nothing I did not already know, and it was a pleasant conversation, but it drove home the point in no uncertain terms that while outside professional investors may care about you and your well-being, what they really are focused on is your company's financial performance relative to the plan that was agreed to when the investment was made.

Investment is not a hobby or avocation for these people. Millions of dollars in investor funds are at stake, and the ability to generate returns for the individual limited partners is the one and only goal. So, as long as you understand that this is the expectation and as long as you can deliver positive results according to your agreement, the investors will work with you. If you can't deliver, for whatever reason, you are at risk that they will choose to cut their losses, and either you or your company might not make it.

However, caveats aside, the infusion of outside capital can be the single biggest factor to accelerate second-stage growth. Here are two powerful success stories involving two different sources of funds.

FOUNDERS BREWING COMPANY

One of the most compelling examples of how outside financing can make the second stage feasible is Founders Brewing Co. Founders Brewing is currently the fastest growing brewer in the United States. For the first ten years of the company's existence, the owners struggled to maintain adequate capital to run the business. The business nearly went bankrupt on more than one occasion. Dave Engbers, one of the founders, remembers spending days dodging creditors and applying for every new credit card he could get his hands on.

Like many small businesses unable to get a material business credit line from a lending institution, Engbers and his cofounder had to resort to personal credit cards despite the double-digit interest costs. By the time they got a new card, it would soon be maxed out to buy grain, hops, packaging materials, and to keep the lights on. Many times he and his cofounder, Mike Stevens, were not able to take a paycheck.

Finally, after ten years in business, they had exhausted the limits of friends and family investors and credit cards. The bank was calling in the loan they had managed to secure years earlier and Engbers' landlord was threatening eviction. It was a dire picture. However, being in essence a manufacturer, Founders had some valuable assets. The founders hoped that banks would see the possible collateral in these assets and loan them the necessary capital. But since profits were elusive and neither of the two founders had personal resources to guarantee a new loan, this option was also off the table.

Dave remembers all too well what he discovered in that critical time. Banks and traditional lending institutions are eager to help the companies that need help the least.

Private equity investors were not a consideration in Founders' financing options as Engbers and his partner did not think the business model was of sufficient scale or adequately proven to meet the requirements of this class of investors. Also, they knew that if they did secure capital from these sources, they would lose control of the company.

At the eleventh hour, the struggling brewery was saved by two high-net-worth investors and a few other coinvestors who believed that Founders Brewing Co. was on to something unique and special. The investors were impressed with the unwavering dedication of the owners, their willingness to sacrifice everything for the products they believed in. One investor, in exchange for an equity stake in the business, personally guaranteed the existing bank debt. Another investor cleared up the overdue rent payments. These investors provided an additional $4 million to fund a move to a new location and to overhaul the company's product line. This infusion of working capital bought enough time for Dave and Mike to execute their new business plan.

Today, Founders Brewing Co. is experiencing wild success. This success has made it possible for Founders Brewing in early 2013 to announce it would open a new $26 million facility for production to keep up with surging demand for its products, a taproom expansion, beer garden, and educational facility.[6] And now, the company has grown enough as a business in revenue and profit to leverage bank debt to fund the expansion.

AXIOM SFD

AXIOM SFD is a Dallas-based sales force training and development firm. In 2009, Bob Sanders returned to the company where he had served earlier as a partner for thirteen years. This time around, he rejoined the firm as president. His explicit mandate was to retool the company from a traditional "butts in the seat" model of providing sales training to a state-of-the-art company that provided a blend of classroom and web-based training as well as a rich library of content and learning tools for both salespeople and sales managers.

However, Bob had some challenges. The company did not have adequate capital to complete the development of the new technology platform. Furthermore, the original founder of the business wanted to take some money off the table and reduce his ownership percentage in the business.

In Bob's view he had two choices. He could continue to invest free cash flow to fund the necessary technology enhancements while keeping adequate reserves as a liquidity hedge in the event the economy reverted to a recessionary condition. This is a tricky balancing act for any small business, and all of us remember the extraordinarily difficult business climate that resulted from the financial crisis in 2008–2009. Furthermore, the current size and profit performance of the company did not really provide adequate capital for Bob to execute the growth plan he believed was correct for capitalizing on the market opportunity in front of him. The other alternative was an outside capital infusion from either a traditional bank or mezzanine lending institution. But AXIOM SFD was still too small to meet the requirements of this category of lender, and moreover, the bank could not address the desire for some liquidity on the part of the original owner.

To fully evaluate his options, Bob retained a financial advisor who suggested he approach private equity firms that might be interested in his new business model. With a new business plan in hand, Bob and his advisor found a private equity firm that was comfortable with a growth capital model, and they struck a deal. This firm, Evolution Capital Partners, which is based in Cleveland, Ohio, actually exists to fund second-stage businesses. As part of the deal with Evolution, AXIOM SFD's original founder received a cash payout for his percentage of the established value of the company at the time of the new investor's capital infusion. Bob received enough new capital to fund the new technology, build the sales organization, and execute a new marketing plan. In the end, equity financing was the best option for AXIOM SFD. The trade-off was that the private equity partner now has majority control of the company.

If the company is successful in executing the new plan, the outside capital will make it possible to transform the company, accelerate growth by over 400 percent in the next five years, increase market share, and create new wealth for many in the company. This last aspect, the potential to create wealth for a broader employee group other than just the two founders, was a very important part of the decision process for Bob. If AXIOM SFD can execute its plan, a sizable part of the team will do well.

PARTING WORDS

For a firm to achieve hypergrowth in the second stage and beyond, it is rare to not require large infusions of capital. Plowing existing profits into development or tapping friends and family will not get you there. Traditional lenders and debt financing can take too long and require financial parameters that your company probably will be unable meet even as a successful start-up. Venture Capital and private investors can provide a very practical option. And while this option is not for everyone, venture capital and private equity firms can work well in certain situations.

In order the find a sufficiently deep-pocketed investment partner, you will need to create a new business plan that clearly defines your timetable, strategic goals, and desired rate of growth. Then the search for capital begins. No approach is perfect. Whether it involves high-net-worth investors, venture capitalists, or private equity firms, every approach essentially ends up as a trade-off between rate of growth and control. There is no free lunch.

Chapter 3

INSTALL A BOARD OF DIRECTORS

ENTREPRENEURS ARE MAVERICKS. Many of them have left the corporate world to pursue their dream of starting their own business. They've put their heart and soul (and money) into their new start-up and made it successful. They're used to making their own rules, doing things their own way. The last thing they want is to have to listen to a board of directors give advice about what they should be doing, right?

Wrong.

Second-stage entrepreneurship requires a new way of thinking about the future of your business. Your goal is to scale the business well beyond its current state. It will take resources and expertise that you most likely don't have. You will need the advice and counsel of a group of individuals who have a wide variety of skills and contacts different from your own and who share your goal of moving your company to the next level. You need to install a board of directors.

A board of directors can provide relevant and complementary expertise, experience, connections, oversight, and often also new capital resources. In a large public company, a board of directors is required by law and rightfully so. The board governs the corporation and has the authority to make the fundamental decisions that guide the company. The board approves the members of the senior management team from the CEO on down to run the company day to day. It is accountable to the shareholders of the corporation and is obligated to protect their interests.

In a private company, assuming there is a board, the structure and governance role of the board varies widely. In most cases, the board of directors is a trusted team of advisors who are there to further the best interests of the company. The ultimate authority for any decision typically lies with the founder and his or her partners. A proactive board provides the guidance and insight to make the management team perform more effectively. This is particularly important in the push to second-stage growth. Think of it as a guardrail on the super-highway to success. A quality board is there to make sure that even though you may scrape against the rails from time to time, you ulti-mately don't leave the road.

The more ambitious the entrepreneur, the sooner he or she will realize the value of creating a board. In fact, most start-ups backed by angel investors or venture capital firms are required by their inves-tors to establish a board as the firm is launched. Having a board of directors indicates a solid business foundation and can attract new resources and larger corporate clients.

For example, in the case of Founders Brewing Co. the original founders came to the conclusion that they were often making deci-sions based mostly on their gut. They knew everything about brew-ing great beer. But once they started to grow, the business became far more complex. They were faced with complicated decisions on matters such as supply chain, real estate, logistics, and multitiered distribution. They were smart enough to realize that they just did not have enough knowledge or experience to make the best calls. So they decided to bring in a board of directors.

Some of the individuals they tapped were the professional inves-tors with a stake in the company whose financial experience was vital to their growth goals. They recruited an executive from the furni-ture industry, a president of a construction company, someone with significant marketing expertise, a successful real estate developer, and last but not least, Dave Engber's father, who was both an accom-plished executive and knew the history of the business from the start. Each board member brought a unique knowledge and skill set that the company would need to grow. In a postscript I want to note that three of the board members have subsequently joined the company in full-time roles.

THE COMPOSITION OF THE BOARD

You will need to assemble a list of the specific skills, expertise, and experience you are looking for in board members. It is always useful to involve your senior management team or partners as well when compiling your list of desired board qualities.

Some qualities of potential board candidates include:

- knowledge of financial management
- knowledge of financing strategies and capital markets
- access to capital resources
- familiarity with legal and government regulations
- knowledge of your industry
- functional knowledge of key aspects of the business, such as sales, marketing, operations, research and design
- industry contacts
- location

These qualifications might sound a bit too aggressive for your first board of directors. They might be. But rest assured that each of these attributes will help your business grow. While no individual board member can provide each of these qualities, you can certainly assemble a group of candidates that share most of them. Just as in the hiring process of new employees, it is important to prioritize which attributes are most important to the kind of board you want for your company.

For instance, access to new capital might trump some of the other concerns in your drive to second-stage growth, and you'll hope to recruit a member who can bring this to the table. If you intend to build a sales force, past experience in scaling a sales organization and establishing sales management processes might be key qualities. The idea is to assemble a team where the skills of the individual board members complement each other and the sum becomes greater than its parts.

In addition to the specific "technical" skills and experience, it is important to consider the human factor when recruiting board members. The candidates need to be able fit into the culture of the business and share your goals. They will be spending a great deal of time with you, your senior management team, and the rest of the board, so the members need to get along with the group.

Each business is unique. It is critical to have board members who understand the essential nature of the business and its goals for short-term and long-term success. Over time, a good board member comes to a very thorough understanding of the mission, strategy, operating plan, and culture of the business. Board members will also get to know some of the key people in the company in addition to the CEO and the senior team. The most effective board members invest time in getting a feel for who works in the company. Digging a little deeper into the day-to-day operations empowers the board to assist the senior team in shaping important initiatives such as policy issues, personnel selection, business development, and the efficient use of resources.

RECRUITING A BOARD

Once you decide to install a board and agree on a list of the criteria you want the board members to meet, how do you go about recruiting the members? Personal contacts? Professional associations or agencies? Word of mouth? Cold calls? All of the above?

Large companies hire specialized executive recruiting firms to handle these searches. This approach certainly works well, but it is not without considerable expense. The best approach for your small company on the rise is to utilize your network of professional contacts. Just as when you had to find private investor groups, you need to get advice from people both within your industry and outside of it. Accountants, lawyers, consultants, private equity professionals, and investment bankers are all connected to individuals who might be suitable candidates. Chances are some people you know or have met in business circles might be potential candidates or know of other people you might approach.

There are also a variety of networking organizations you can tap into for little to no cost that have a roster of suitable individuals. For example, in Chicago there is an organization called Boardroom Bound. This organization identifies and develops board candidates. It has a database of diverse, highly qualified individuals from many different industries that have expressed serious interest in joining a board of directors.

If your business is local in its focus, it probably makes sense to recruit board members who live in the general area where your business is located. This keeps things simple. However, if your business is national or international in its focus or operations, then having individuals from outside your locale makes sense. A good board should also be as diverse a group as possible. Not only does diversity help to capture the full span of the concerns of your customer base and overall market, it also inspires more expansive thinking from a variety of perspectives.

There is no set general rule for the ideal size of a board. I have seen very small boards of three or four individuals work well. I have also been part of a highly effective board that had more than ten members. The size of the board depends on what guidance you need to accelerate your company to second-stage success. A solid goal for most small companies is to assemble a board of four to six outside members. This number will give you enough intellectual horsepower and business expertise to guide the CEO and the management team to grow your company.

COMPENSATING THE BOARD

For most individuals who agree to join the board of a small private company, compensation is usually not their primary motivation.

Maybe they find the strategy and mission of the company compelling, and they want to be part of the story and help turbocharge the potential for success. Maybe they have achieved success and accumulated enough wealth to retire, but want to keep active in an advisory capacity. Perhaps they are investors in the business and want to make sure their interests are protected. However, no matter what the personal motivation of a potential board member is, all of them are business professionals and the issue of compensation for their time and service will need to be addressed.

As you can imagine, there are dozens of ways to set up compensation. Aside from the amount of company resources available, one of the most important factors is the extent of the commitment you require from the board members. Will they have decision-making and voting powers or serve as trusted but nonvoting advisors? How many formal meetings will they be required to attend? Will the service require travel time and who will pay for the arrangements? How much input will they be required to provide and what form will it take? You will need to decide the scope of the board's responsibilities and the appropriate package you can offer. Usually, compensation is a topic that will be included in the recruitment pitch. All board members should receive the same compensation for their service, as this will help avoid potentially uncomfortable conversations down the road when the specifics of every board member's arrangement become known.

In addition to the amount of the compensation package, what form the compensation will take is an important decision as well. For instance, if your company is a start-up or is actively engaged in second-stage growth, a package involving cash payments might not be practical. Capital is a precious commodity especially when you're planning new growth. Even a nominal fee per meeting or a yearly stipend can take a big bite out of your budget.

Equity is a more common and affordable approach to compensation for new companies. It requires no out-of-pocket expense and aligns the interests of the board members with those of the management team who are trying to build significant equity value over time. A typical allocation for a board member of a modestly sized private company is .5 to 1.0 percent of the common equity, typically vesting in three or four years. If equity vesting schedules are already in place for management, you should use the same amortization schedules for board members. The percentage allocation of equity may vary inversely depending on the size of your company.

Public companies offer far richer board compensation packages than the amount mentioned above. They also require much more time and effort than what you will require, and they are not without real risk. Nonetheless, be sure to take this into consideration if you are targeting candidates who sit on the boards of public companies. You may have real trouble recruiting them if compensation is their primary motive for joining your board.

ENGAGING THE BOARD

Once you have a board in place, you then have to find the best way to interact with the board members individually and as a whole. Consistent and regular official communication along with informal events are the best practice to keep the board informed, engaged, and motivated to support the best interests of your company.

The formal communications can take the form of monthly or quarterly meetings during which the board gathers with the senior team to discuss the prior period's performance, outlook for the period ahead, and most important, some of the key decisions the company faces concerning future growth.

These formal gatherings need to be treated as such. Attendance at these meetings must be a requirement of service. Each meeting should last at least a half day. Given the current sophistication of virtual meeting technology, you'll need to decide whether virtual attendance is appropriate. My view is that face-to-face meetings are far preferable. Make sure you arrange for a suitable professional space to hold the meetings. If the board members are located some distance from the meeting place, travel arrangements need to be taken into consideration as well.

The frequency of board meetings depends on the individuals on the board, on their willingness and ability to invest time, and on the needs of the business. The standard approach tends to be to meet quarterly. In a second-stage business, things can change quickly and even a quarterly meeting might not be sufficiently frequent to address the immediate needs quickly enough. If the company is growing rapidly, the best practice might be a combination of in-person quarterly meetings and strategic monthly meetings by teleconference or Skype to address pressing issues in real time. The management team and the board need to decide what works best for the company.

It is important for the management team (and for the board members) to properly prepare for all board meetings. The team should produce a written agenda and presentation for all board meetings whether face-to-face, by phone, or via virtual screen technology. Don't try to cover too much on the agenda at any one meeting. The presentation materials for the meetings should be delivered to each member in advance. The materials should be comprehensive enough for the board member to grasp the issues at hand, formulate questions, and come to the meeting fully prepared to discuss them thoroughly. Keep the board materials to the point and appropriately succinct. Few board members have the time or inclination to digest a 60-page PowerPoint board presentation.

The point of allocating half a day for a formal quarterly board meeting is to allow for adequate time to cover a few topics in sufficiently detailed fashion to get at the heart of the issues at hand. In this way, the discussion and analysis are much more likely to get at the core of the problem and provide concrete solutions to the management team. Monthly calls are more tactical in nature, typically reviewing progress against the annual operating and financial plan and discussing corrective action for specific issues that surface between the quarterly meetings.

The informal events and discussions are also quite valuable in many ways, perhaps even more so than formal sessions. Casual social gatherings such as dinner or drinks with board members and senior managers, if physically possible, go a long way toward cementing relationships. An occasional phone call or email or Skype check-in also help to create a sense of collegiality as well. Other informal events such as year-end company-wide parties or a tour of the offices or facilities each year help the board understand the operations and meet the staff. Make sure the board knows that it has access to you and your team to ask questions or make an informal comment. Staying in touch is the best way to underscore the board members' importance to the company and its future.

This may sound time-consuming, but you'll find it is time well spent. The board is an integral part of your company. You've chosen its members carefully and want to make sure they are working at peak capacity in the interests of your business. Making the effort to keep them in the loop, solicit their thoughts and opinions, and seriously consider their solid business expertise all serve to improve your company and make it grow.

TALES FROM THE BOARD ROOM

Each of the companies I have been part of or started used seed capital from private equity firms. The establishment of a board of directors was a condition for the funding, so we had a board in place from the day we opened the doors. Initially, the board was comprised of the CEO and several individuals from the venture capital or private equity firm. As the company established critical mass, and the business model began to prove itself, we decided to expand the board and recruit new members whose experience filled some gaps that existed between the management team and the private equity firm's board members. For example, at Alternative Resources Corporation, we added an executive from the Johnson Wax Company who had significant experience in marketing because we wanted to add knowledge of that aspect of the business. We also added a retired Xerox sales executive who had a long career in leading very large selling organizations.

At Parson Group, building an all-star board was part of the strategy to build credibility in the company brand and to assist a young and relatively inexperienced management team. This recruitment strategy, while requiring a significant investment, proved to be invaluable in accelerating growth. When we called on our primary customer targets, CFOs, we touted the blue-chip credentials of our board of directors as evidence that if Parson had the support of industry titans, its services were impeccable, and they were taking minimal risk by deciding to use a start-up firm in a critical area of their firm.

We also heavily leveraged the skills, contacts, and experience of these seasoned board members by engaging them in informal talks on their schedule. One board member, a Harvard Business School professor named Gary Loveman, called me to talk nearly every Saturday afternoon. That was the best time for him to talk, and it certainly worked well for me.

Another board member invited me to his house for coffee once a month, and we would spend a couple of hours talking about the business and my performance running the business. At the time, this particular individual, Don Perkins, also served on the boards of AT&T, Time Warner, Cummins Engine, and Putnam Funds. I was very grateful to have an opportunity to talk with such an experienced and capable individual on a regular basis who was also the former chairman and CEO of one of the nation's larger food retailers.

Two other members who happened to be the co-chairmen of the Parson Group board had many contacts in a variety of industries and were especially well connected in Chicago. These two board members, Jeff Louis and Sam Chapman, became high-profile figures in the company and participated in nearly all of the management and training sessions we conducted for the staff. They knew virtually every person in the company by name. In addition to providing the initial capital for the firm at its founding, they reinforced the culture we built and rightfully deserve a ton of credit for some of the success we came to enjoy.

Despite their stature and busy schedules, our board members agreed to take part in an experiment. Each of the board members volunteered to serve as a mentor to one of the members of our senior team. They would have a regular monthly meeting with their mentee and remain accessible to that person by phone during business hours. We encouraged our team to take advantage of the board members' wealth of experience and knowledge to enhance their performance and pursue any networking possibilities they offered to broaden our client base. In addition to being of real value to each of the senior executives, it had the added benefit of providing the board members a deeper level of insight on the strategy and operations of the company.

I mentioned Shiftgig in an earlier chapter. As Shiftgig closed on the Series A financing, Eddie Lou made a decision to also establish a board. The conditions of the financing did not require this. Eddie, with his venture capital background, is well versed on the advantages that a good board can provide and decided the company would benefit enormously from establishing a board early on. The Shiftgig board includes some big names from the technology industry, among them Match.com CEO Sam Yagan, Brian Spaly, the CEO of Chicago-based men's clothing distributor Trunk Club, and Ken Pelletier, former CTO of Groupon; the latter serves as a technical advisor. However, these people were not picked for their "big names." Instead, each of the board members was selected to fill a needed role in helping the management team of Shiftgig capitalize on the market opportunity they believe is in front of them.

Sam Yagan has successfully started and scaled three different Internet companies. He has a strong point of view on how to deliver rapid growth in this space. Further, he has been successful raising money for these businesses without tapping the institutional market, instead choosing angel and high-net worth investor partners. Brian Spaly has started and scaled two online retailers. As opposed to Sam's approach, Brian financed his companies through funding provided by institutional venture investors. Brian is also an expert of sorts in the world of sales, an area of expertise that Eddie wanted to shore up. Ken Pelletier, as the former CTO for Groupon, one of the fastest growing companies of any kind in corporate history, knows a thing or two about building and scaling technology infrastructure in high-growth situations. Sean Casey, currently one of the cofounders of Shiftgig and also its CTO, is also on the board. Sean has previous experience starting a technology firm.

Eddie will tell you that he very thoughtfully and carefully put together his board to provide expertise in three areas. He wanted help and experience from those who had previously successfully scaled technology businesses. He also wanted to be able to get advice from a board with experience in getting financing from angel investors and from institutional investors. Both are important, as the optimal path for Shiftgig in its future financing needs is still uncertain. Finally, all companies ultimately have to "sell," to both their internal and external markets, and Brian's experience in online retailing fills a needed gap as he has extensive experience in sales.

All of the Shiftgig directors are local to Chicago. Eddie thought this was important in that the geographic proximity provides easy access to all these individuals. There are, of course, formal meetings, but a great deal of the value of this board comes from the informal communication and spontaneous meetings that occur between the formal meetings. With everyone in the same city, this is much easier to arrange.

The compensation for this team is entirely equity based. Like the management team, the board members want to be part of growing an exciting new company that grows by filling a unique need in the market. It is still early in the journey for Shiftgig, but they are off to an impressive start.

PARTING WORDS

As a savvy second-stage entrepreneur, you need to recognize when you alone can't take your company to the next level. There are skills and networks that you will need, and the best way to get them is to install a board of directors. Prioritize the qualities you want in your board members. Explore all avenues to target the best, most experienced business professionals you can afford and get them on board as quickly as possible.

At the end of the day, a good board is supportive of the management team but does not refrain from asking tough questions when such questions are warranted. While they may not always act as "gadflies" to spur creative solutions, they won't be afraid to play devil's advocate if it will help challenge the company to grow and prosper.

The best boards challenge the members of the management team to push themselves, to think about alternatives they perhaps dismissed, and will hold management accountable for executing strategies and plans effectively. A good board makes a good management team better.

Chapter 4

CREATE, DON'T COMPETE

BUILD A BETTER MOUSETRAP. For most people, this is just another tired cliché we've all heard a thousand times. But to entrepreneurs, it's a rallying cry. Whether they are frustrated by the lack of quality coffee or by the agonizingly slow hiring process in most companies or by a significant market need that is left unfulfilled, they have a vision about how to provide something different, something unique, something better, and they seize the opportunity—and make money doing it.

Creativity is the foundation of startup businesses. Entrepreneurs look at existing products or services from a different perspective and turn them inside out to create something customers can't live without. Inspired and passionate about their mission to capitalize on their personal vision, they start their own business to make their dream a reality.

To build a better mousetrap, many start with the old trap and then fundamentally improve it. The Milwaukee-based company HarQen is a great example of entrepreneurial creativity. Kelly and Jeff Fitzsimmons founded ComicWonder, a company that offered an ad-supported free online service for customers to record jokes over the phone and then email the recordings to their friends. It was a popular and unique service that relied on a new web technology platform. But after a few years, the business wasn't growing fast enough. The business model was too dependent on a limited base of appropriate advertisers.

Then, the entrepreneurs got creative. How could they use this terrific technology platform to provide a fee-based service? What industry could benefit most from this kind of service? Then it hit them: the recruitment function in the corporate world. A big part of the job of corporate recruiters is to screen applicants who look promising on paper by phone, the goal being to take a large pool of candidates and narrow this down to a smaller, more qualified group. It takes costly man-hours playing phone tag, setting up mutually agreeable times, then conducting the screening interview and taking notes. Further, even if you discover in the second minute that the person you are talking to is for some reason not a good fit, you risk impairment to your brand if you abruptly end the phone call. Instead, done with respect and some politeness, it typically requires 10 to 15 minutes to conduct each phone screening call. The process is inefficient, cumbersome, and prone to error.

The Fitzsimmonses saw an opportunity and adapted their existing technology to create a system that automated the entire screening interview process. Instead of arranging the phone calls themselves for suitable applicants, the recruiters directed them to a confidential website where the applicants would answer a series of questions by calling a special number and recording their voice answers. The "interview" could be at any time, day or night, at the convenience of the applicant. The recruiters could then review these interviews on their own schedule as well, easily sifting through them to create a pool of qualified candidates and doing follow-up. Using this technology, unqualified candidates can be dealt with in a minute or two, with computer generated email responses to candidates handling the process in a professional fashion. In 2007, the entrepreneurs' new company, HarQen, was born. In 2010, this product, called VoiceAdvantage, was voted "Product of the Year" by *Human Resource Executive* magazine. A market leader, it continues to grow in revenue and new clients each year.

HarQen's success story and the hundreds of others like it are based on innovation. Every business, no matter its stage of development, will benefit from tapping into the creative energy that differentiated the company from the competition from the start. Your start-up built its success on the fresh product or service it offered to a market hungry for it. In order to continue that momentum and drive your business to second-stage growth and beyond: *create, don't compete.*

Going head-to-head with your competitors with the same products, competing for the same customers is a costly strategy that never delivers adequate ROI and certainly won't grow your business. Large companies can afford to invest millions on marketing their products, often squeezing out smaller businesses. Competing on price only eats into your profitability and is not sustainable. Promoting your products as higher quality or your customer service as more user-friendly and efficient than that of your competitors helps differentiate your business but will only get the company so far. At the end of the day, you may find yourself running in place or even losing ground.

Go back to basics. Ask yourself why did you start your business in the first place? What made your products or services unique and drove your initial success? You need to rediscover and reapply that start-up mentality to reinvigorate your company and catapult it to the second stage of growth. To paraphrase the old sports idiom: The best defense is a creative offense.

No matter what the business, to achieve second-stage growth you need to stay at the top of your creative game. You must take a fresh look at your market. What's missing from the current scheme that your company can offer? It may mean expanding the current offerings with new and exciting products to meet the changing marketplace. It may mean building on core expertise and extending it into new, underserviced niches. It may mean changing the fundamental way in which an industry operates. The more creative you are, the less you'll need to worry about your competitors.

This strategy—create, don't compete—takes ingenuity. It is more than a simple repackaging of existing products that incorporates all kinds of bells and whistles or slick incentives. Remember, you don't have to start from scratch. After all, you've already had some level of success. You have to be creative about using what you have to get where you want to be.

Few industries are as adept at using innovation to accelerate growth as technology companies. Dozens of tech startups, such as Groupon, Snapchat, Amazon, Salesforce.com, Facebook, Twitter, LinkedIn, and EBay, demonstrate the power of innovation to spur growth. They have changed the world and the way we do business. Even though they are all relatively new, it has become difficult to remember when these companies didn't exist.

Probably one of the most dramatic and best known examples of a company that built its growth on the principle of create, don't compete is Apple, Inc. Steve Jobs, Steve Wozniak, and Ronald Wayne had an idea that would revolutionize the personal computer business. With the eventual launch of the Macintosh, they created a unique operating system that was so user friendly that it demystified personal computers. Supported by attractively designed products that captured the consumers' imagination, the three founders' "upstart" start-up took off. Since that humble beginning, the entrepreneurs have shown an amazing ability to innovate, creating exciting new inventions like the iPod, iPhone, iPad along with upgrades and ongoing redesigns of their entire line of personal computer products. Apple has demonstrated an ability not only to stay ahead of the curve, but it has created the market for others to follow.

However, most of us are not tech entrepreneurs. We do business in traditional markets less driven by lightning-fast innovation. But the principle holds up just as well. Even in the most established industries, with razor-thin margins and price-conscious customers, innovation can catapult a successful start-up to hypergrowth. Let's take a look at a few businesses that achieved success by innovation.

INTELLIGENTSIA COFFEE AND TEA

Many may think that with the tremendous success of companies such as Starbucks, Peets, and Caribou, the opportunity in the upscale coffee retailing industry is long gone. After all, Starbucks has created a

global empire, with retail outlets on nearly every corner and a ubiq-
uitous brand that almost defines gourmet coffee. How could any
start-up hope to be successful in the shadow of this giant in a market already fragmented with other contenders?

Doug Zell founded Intelligentsia Coffee and Tea in 1995 because
of his passion for a superlative cup of coffee. He loved every aspect of
the coffee experience: from roasting the beans to the careful preparation and serving of each cup. He had his own vision about how to
bring the ultimate coffee experience to serious coffee lovers in his
hometown of Chicago, so he opened his own shop.

The goal at the time was to provide great coffee to customers by
personally roasting the best beans available on the premises, grind-
ing them a little at a time, then brewing the coffee according to Doug
Zell's painstaking personal standard.

Never satisfied, he experimented with his product constantly. When
the beans he got from wholesalers weren't of high enough quality, he
went directly to the growers themselves. When the high-tech coffee
urns used by every other store didn't deliver the taste he wanted, he
created an entirely new system that everyone thought would sink his
fledging retail store: preparing each cup of coffee by hand.

Doug's creative approach to delivering the highest quality coffee paid off. Nothing available in retail gourmet coffee market even
came close to the taste of Intelligentsia coffee. Word spread, and soon
there were lines out the door. His little shop on Broadway in the then
somewhat seedy north side of Chicago had become *the* destination
for coffee lovers. As his concept proved itself beyond all expectations,
he expanded his roasting and retail operations. All these years later,
his company has grown to over 300 employees with retail locations in
multiple cities and wholesale customers for their beans nationwide.

Now one of the most respected coffee experts in the world, Doug
continues to innovate. In contrast to the cookie-cutter look of his
competitors' outlets, each Intelligentsia coffee emporium has its own

distinct design. He is one of the few artisan coffee sellers to source 100 percent of his beans directly from growers at direct and fair market prices, ensuring the highest quality available. His ongoing innovative approach continues to bear out his strategy of "create, don't compete."

WHOLE FOODS MARKET

The concept of the supermarket has been with us since the early 1900s. Clarence Saunders invented the self-service market when he opened his first Piggly Wiggly store in Memphis, Tennessee, in 1916. The idea spread quickly and became the industry standard to the present day. National chains began to dominate the market. As their market share grew and the stores multiplied, the packaged food producers created the products to fill the chains' shelves.

But in the 1970s, a small segment of the American population started to become more health conscious and a sliver of the consumer food market started to shift away from prepackaged items filled with chemicals to organic and fresh foods. The supermarket model was not built for stocking these higher-priced items in part because they lacked preservatives and had a shorter shelf life. Consumers interested in buying these foods had to search out the small organic markets and fruit stands that were just beginning to spring up around metropolitan centers all over the country. This was time-consuming and expensive. For suburbanites, this option was virtually nonexistent.

In 1978, John Mackey opened a small natural foods market in Austin, Texas, named SaferWay. Two years later, looking to meet the increasing demand of the growing market for better foods, he partnered with Craig Weller and Mark Skiles to merge SaferWay with their Clarksville Natural Grocery, creating the first Whole Foods Market. Patterning itself on the supermarket model, their innovation was the product mix they offered: a large selection of organic food, both fresh and packaged, including cheese, milk, meat, fish, fruits, and vegetables. They sold the highest quality items and charged a premium price for them for the convenience of providing them in one location.

Whole Foods Market created a new kind of supermarket perfectly suited to the changing tastes of America. Over the next six years, the company expanded to six stores in Texas and Louisiana. The rest is history. Today, Whole Foods Market has 321 stores in the United States and the United Kingdom and annual revenues exceeding $10 billion.[1] Whole Foods continues to innovate, not content to rest on past successes. The stores' prepared food section continues to grow in both size and variety of options available to the shopper, and these prepared foods can be taken home or consumed in the store where the company has added tables, chairs, and seats at the bar. The owners' emphasis on fine wine options, including a variety of tastings, attracts people to the stores for a more social arrangement. In urban areas, Whole Foods is often one of the early pioneers to locate a new store in a neighborhood undergoing gentrification, and the company's presence certainly spurs the process along.

NEXT

The high-end restaurant industry caters to the upscale foodie market. These customers demand not only the highest quality of food, impeccably prepared, but also the latest trends in gourmet dining. Exotic meats from the around the globe and state-of-the-art techniques are the hallmarks. Innovative cuisine is the guiding force of fine dining establishments. However, the basic business model has remained the same for many years. The customer reserves a seat in the restaurant, chooses from the menu that often changes daily, and pays for the meal at the end. While some restaurants don't take reservations or offer only prix fixe menus, the basic business model remains the same.

However, even in this time-tested, traditional industry, creativity still can lead to success, as has been proven by an establishment in Chicago called Next. Acclaimed chef/restaurateur Grant Achatz built a national reputation for brilliance after opening his three-star Alinea restaurant in Chicago in 2005.[2] Alinea is currently ranked by *Restaurant Magazine* as the best restaurant in North America and the sixth best dining establishment in the world.[3] Building on his successful start-up, Achatz turned the model for fine dining on its head with two innovations when he launched Next in 2011. First, instead of changing his menu daily, he offers a new themed menu at various times during a year. His themes are uniquely enigmatic, such as "Paris, 1906," "The Hunt," "Sicily," "Vegan." or "A Tour of Thailand."[4]

But the true innovation that took the fining dining crowd by storm was how his customers take part in the dining experience. Rather than follow the usual reservation/pay-as-you-exit model, Next follows a model similar to the online travel or entertainment industries. Diners need to buy a "ticket" online in advance. The prices vary according to the time of day and day of the week. All food and beverages, including preselected wine pairings and service charges, are billed in advance. Tickets are quite expensive and nonrefundable. Demand has been so strong that tickets are gone nearly instantly after release each week. Currently, tickets for Next can be found on craigslist at $500 each. Chef Achatz has another hit on his hands and may have fundamentally changed the business model for fine dining. This is Chef Achatz's second huge success, and it is unlikely he will stop here.

SOULCYCLE

Unless you happen to live in Los Angeles or New York City, it is unlikely that you have heard of SoulCycle. SoulCycle was started in 2006 by Elizabeth Cutler, Julie Rice, and Ruth Zukerman (Ruth left the company in 2009 to start a competitor). Their first location was in a former funeral home on the Upper West Side in Manhattan. On the surface, SoulCycle is not so unique. It is a place where you can take a spinning class. However, what Cutler and Rice have done to build SoulCycle into a cult sensation is brilliant. The experience of SoulCycle is unique. Each class is matched with an instructor who is specifically targeted to appeal to the demographic group likely to attend that class. For example, there is a big difference between who attends a class at 11:00 a.m. and 7:30 p.m., and the instructors who are slated to teach in those respective slots. *New York* magazine called a class at SoulCycle "an experience: part dance party, part therapy, part communal high."[5] As in Bikram Yoga, the heat is turned up high, causing the participants to sweat heavily while spinning. The room is very dark. Unlike in yoga, the music is very loud, and riders are supposed to pedal to the music. The overall experience of attending a SoulCycle class has created a cult phenomenon. Classes sell out quickly as demand exceeds supply.[6] The owners charge $34 for a 45-minute class; thus, after a couple classes you could have funded as much as an entire month's membership in many health clubs. Nonetheless, the success of the concept has driven dramatic growth. The company has 14 locations in New York and Los Angeles.[7] To the credit of the founders, they have taken a concept that has been around for years and reinvented the experience in a fundamental way. Recently, SoulCycle announced a strategic partnership agreement with Equinox, a high-end nationwide health club chain. Together with Equinox, the SoulCycle owners plan to open an additional 70 SoulCycle locations in the near term in two major US cities and in London.[8]

PARSON GROUP

In 1995, my partners and I founded Parson Group to service the financial and accounting service fields in an entirely new way. At the time, if a company needed to outsource its financial services, there were two options open to them: temporary staffing agencies that typically provided support for low-end needs, such as help in accounts payable or accounts receivable, or one of the large and premium-priced public accounting firms. Parson Group offered a fresh and unique proposition: a pool of seasoned, high-quality finance professionals to provide consistent, high-quality services without the high price tag.

Parson Group professionals delivered top-level technical skills coupled with years of experience in the business world to yield pragmatic, concrete attention to a company's financial challenges. Unlike temporary staffing firms that tended to place unemployed finance and accounting professionals as temporary hourly workers as a bridge to full-time employment, Parson Group actually hired the majority of their consultants as full-time, salaried professionals with benefits. Even when selling staffing services, we positioned them as "consulting services" with an accompanying "scope of work" document; that is, we were willing to accept responsibility for a deliverable. Unlike public accounting firms, we didn't offer services such as audit opinions, tax preparation, or verification of financial statements. Our goal was to create a long-lasting relationship with our clients that went beyond simple number crunching.

Parson Group pioneered an entirely new category of finance and accounting service firm that offered consistent quality by experienced professionals that clients could count on for the long term. However, in our early days, we had no brand, reputation, "deal flow," or sufficient capital to compete through brand-building efforts such as advertising and saturation marketing. Our growth strategy was to assemble a highly professional sales organization, reinforced with sales support experts and divided into regional teams. Each person and team in each region was tasked with developing new contacts at Fortune 1000 companies and turn them into clients over a five-year period.

We had to create to compete against both ends of well-established competition. Temporary staffing firms offered less expensive, short-lived services to companies. The reputation for quality varies considerably, but in most cases a staffing firm is not set up to consistently deliver quality outcomes. Public accounting firms relied primarily on partners to bring in lucrative accounts by trading on their high-profile brands and targeting their networks of high-level executives. Public accounting firms have an additional advantage in that much of the work they perform is driven by regulatory compliance. Public accounting firms have typically delivered quality outcomes for their clients, but this comes with a price. Our strategy was totally different. We offered blue-chip services to solve complex financial challenges at reasonable fees.

Our sales people established relationships throughout the finance and accounting industry, targeting all managers and executives responsible for actually providing financial service solutions for their organizations. We believed that building these relationships would ultimately result in revenue.

We encouraged them to develop relationships on a more personal level. They were trained to begin the sales process with regular, informational, phone calls, offering insight and help, with the real goal to set a face-to-face meeting. Our sales people were schooled to have conversations of sufficient depth so that they could understand client needs well beyond the surface level as well as the priorities of those needs. We talked about how we could help and how other organizations with similar issues met their challenges—of course, with our help. Once the relationship was established, then nurtured, we knew that it would be a matter of time before the client requested our specific assistance.

This creative integrated approach paid off. Parson Group grew from a start-up with a relatively small initial capitalization of $4 million to a business with a run rate of over $90 million in the next six years. In our sixth year of operation, *Inc.* magazine ranked Parson Group as the number one fastest growing private company in the United States. Our margins were well over 40 percent compared to less than 20 percent in the traditional staffing industry. We were able to retain and grow our relationships with clients with a degree of loyalty uncommon in the financial services industry.

PARTING WORDS

Regardless of the industry you're in, you may often feel as though there is nothing new under the sun, that your company is chasing the same markets, in the same ways, doing the same things, at the same time as others. But if you fall into that circular thinking, you'll never push past your start-up business into second-stage success.

Just look around at all the start-ups that have made it big. Think about those on the high-growth path today, albeit at an earlier stage. In almost every case, each has made its mark by delivering something new, something fresh. Then, when the market was right, each pushed forward, extending its brand, building on its creativity to offer innovative products in new and exciting ways.

What's exciting about creativity is that sometimes it simply means looking at things differently and using your entrepreneur's spirit to fill a need in a way no one else is creative enough to see. Perhaps like HarQen or Next, Inc., you'll be a trailblazer and change the fundamental paradigm of the way an industry functions and outperform your competitors. Perhaps you'll get down to basics and rely on high-quality creative products, as Intelligentsia Coffee and Teas did, and deliver them in a unique way to propel you to second-stage growth. Whatever creative path you take, the evidence is overwhelming that to become a second-stage entrepreneur you need to remember: create, don't compete.

Chapter 5

HIRING SMART!

STAFFING TO SCALE IS ONE OF THE most important steps to ensure your success for your second-stage company. The real challenge, and the opportunity, is to find people who have the right combination of skills, experience, and passion to succeed that is needed to help you grow your business.

When planning second-stage success, it's easy to focus on the product or the service. After all, that's what the market wants and what drives the revenue, right? While the product is what you market and sell, equally important is the talent of your organization that is responsible for getting the goods to the customer. When you walk in the door of a Starbucks café, it's because you like their products. But what about the three baristas who took the order, capped off the hot milk at just the right time, made sure it was a vente, not a grande, and served it with a smile? What about the R & D team that came up with the winning blends, the titles, and the logo designs? What about the design team that created the welcoming ambience of the Starbucks café?

The fact is, no matter how your company may be identified in the marketplace: its products, its service, its advertising, its engineering, even its commitment to the environment or social causes, it is ultimately the people behind these high-profile characteristics who make the organization great. As Jim Collins so adeptly pointed out in his bestseller *Good to Great*, "it's getting the right people into the right roles doing the right things."[1]

Getting it right the first time around will enable to you achieve your second-stage growth according to plan. False starts will cost time and money and slow the company down. As you plan to expand, you know that you will need to add additional staff. But don't just jump into hiring people to fill the positions you think you'll need.

You have to ask some fundamental questions first, including the following:

- How much capital does the new business plan allocate for personnel expansion?
- How is the staffing budget broken out? By department? By management versus staff?
- What is the proportion of estimated new hires to existing personnel?
- Will expansion require promoting existing high performers to manage an expanded team?
- How many current employees will need to be cut?
- How much will changes to existing staff cost?

Once you target the number and nature of the new staff you'll need, then you can focus on creating a program that will get you the best people.

TALENT MATTERS

A number of years ago, Peter Capelli, George W. Taylor Professor of Management at Wharton, conducted a study concerning employee performance.[2] He found that top-tier talent delivered six to ten times the results compared to average talent, and in highly complex environments, average talent could not deliver results at all. Matt Dixon and Brent Adamson, in their 2011 book entitled *The Challenger Sale*, point out that in research conducted by the Sales Executive Council, its members reported a performance delta of over 200 percent between their stars and core talent.[3] Experienced private equity investors grasp this equation better than most. Their years in the trenches managing their portfolio companies has cemented in their brain that a top-tier management team produces an end result that is easily ten times what is delivered by a second-tier management team.

The evidence corroborates what any experienced manager can tell you: hiring the right people for the right job at the right time pays big dividends. A 2005 HBS study showed that firms with effective leadership performed 40 percent better than firms with average leadership. Additionally, a recent Towers Watson study demonstrated that firms with superior human capital practices create twice the shareholder value as firms with average human capital practices.

Talent is the most important attribute for new hires. But what does "talent" mean in the context of your business? Is it different for each position? How do you sort through applicants to find the best ones? These are all important questions that point to the difficulty inherent in the hiring process.

THE HUMAN CAPITAL EQUATION

While the hiring process remains one of the most important factors in the second stage, it is often the least disciplined, least objective, and least quantifiable process in any business. Despite all of the empirical data, despite all of the intuitive understanding of this issue, hiring top talent remains a mystery to most business leaders, regardless of the size of their company. Of course, there are exceptions to this neglect of such a crucial area, and some companies, such as Google or McKinsey, have somewhat legendary recruitment practices, with the discipline to match. It was once estimated that between screening, interviewing, and assessing, Google invested 87 people-hours on each person hired.[4] But for most second-stage companies, the bar is considerably lower.

Let me provide a simple example to illustrate this point. A company plans to put in a new general ledger system or ERP system. This is a significant investment of time, energy, resources and, of course, capital. For a second-stage company, this could easily be a $1 million decision.

Most businesses, even relatively small ones, will correctly go through a complicated but transparent process to select the proper system. The steps in the process typically include the following:

- Hire a specialized consulting firm to evaluate the parameters of the nature and qualities of the new system need.
- Document current and future state processes.
- Document user requirements.
- Examine system requirements.
- Calculate costs and benefits.
- Document appropriate vendors.
- Check vendor references.
- Arrange vendor interviews and demos.
- Consult Gartner's and International Data Corporation's research on the vendor.

At the end of the process, a vendor is recommended. There are final presentations, and the CEO and/or the executive directly in charge of this system signs off on the decision. Many people are involved, having lots of meetings, sharing extensive analysis, creating endless message streams and paper trails, because this is a critical decision that will impact the company for years to come, and the decision also involves a significant investment.

However, when it comes to hiring, it is rare that the same rigor and discipline are followed even though the investment can be equally (or likely more) significant and the probable impact on the future of the business is far greater. In most business-to-business sales organizations, the hiring of each business development person is at least a $1 million decision. For each first level manager role the investment value is significantly higher, easily exceeding $10 million. Senior leadership roles have ever greater value—or cost—if you happen to get the hiring wrong. Unless there is a dedicated recruiting function within the company, the hiring manager is pretty much left on his or her own to find, sort, interview, vet, and finally select applicants. Even if there is an in-house HR recruitment function, the way the process actually works is quite a bit different from the theory of how it should operate—and that difference is not good.

Often someone is recommended for hire based on a gut level instinct or subjective factors, such as being a fellow graduate of the hiring manager's college, having an effervescent personality, or being recommended by a fellow employee who happens to be a friend of the applicant. It is not an infrequent occurrence for an entrepreneur just embarking on a second-stage path to hire a person for a critical role without talking to a single other candidate.

If done correctly, the hiring process takes time. Busy entrepreneurs or hiring managers often can't spare the time and attention it takes to sift through a list of well-qualified candidates. Often the screening is left up to a recruiter who doesn't really understand the parameters of the position or lacks the experience or knowledge to properly vet the candidate. Interviews are conducted hastily and without appropriate depth. Even when training on effective interviewing is provided, many hiring managers do not have the discipline or inclination to follow the process.

Much of the research available for this process suggests that an interviewer essentially decides in the first two minutes (or less) of the interview whether the candidate is someone they "like." It is at that point that the interview needs to drill down, probing the candidate for his or her experience and what he or she will bring to the position. However, often the tenor of the interview shifts quickly from probing the candidate to selling him or her on the position. The fact is that many hiring managers like to talk rather than conduct a probing interview in a disciplined fashion.

When hiring managers present the candidate of choice to the decision makers, they spend their time trying to "pump up" a candidate's credentials to support their choice rather than present the pros and cons of the hiring decision objectively.

You get the idea. Current hiring practices are neither disciplined nor quantified processes. While this is often true in the large corporate world, it is even more often the case in start-ups seeking to move to the second stage of development on a tight time line. Initially, everyone from the founder on down is wearing multiple hats. All employees have been making many decisions by intuition and gut feeling, and since the business has achieved success, there's no reason to change regarding the hiring process. While both of these subjective qualities are important and do in fact play a critical role in the hiring process, they have to be tempered by discipline and structure. To succeed in assembling the right employees who will propel your business forward, you need to learn how to hire smart.

THE FOUR PRINCIPLES OF HIRING SMART

Hiring talented, top-tier people with the potential to grow with the company is the goal of any leader or manager. But how do you define talent in the context of the specific position? How do you recognize it in a candidate? Just as you have to ask the big questions when deciding to expand your staff, you need to ask pointed questions to implement the expansion including the following:

- Should one value experience over potential?
- Do you have adequate training resources to bring the less experienced new hire up to speed quickly?
- How important are academic credentials?
- Do you hire age and wisdom over youth and enthusiasm?
- How much can you rely on the candidate's past success?

- What if a person has worked for you before in a different firm or in a different capacity in the same firm?
- How important is fitting in with the company culture?

We all want to hire smart, especially when the company is on a growth path. But so many other factors come into play that we often sacrifice due diligence for expediency. Recruitment industry metrics that are known as the "time to fill" and "cost to fill" factors often overtake the "quality of the fill" that gets measured in the hiring process. Costly mistakes are made and everyone suffers as a consequence.

To take the guesswork out of the process, I have developed four principles to guide you to success when making hiring decisions. Based on decades of recruiting, hiring, and retaining high-performing personnel, these principles will improve your odds of assembling the top-tier talent you need to move your company to second-stage success.

PRINCIPLE ONE: DEFINE THE JOB AND THE SELECTION CRITERIA

Before beginning a search for the perfect candidates to fill needed roles, you need to define each position in terms of its specific goals and responsibilities. If it is an existing position, be sure to reassess its parameters in the context of the push to expand into second-stage success. If it is a new position, be sure to think long and hard about what is required and how this fits into the new organizational structure designed to promote growth. The job definition should be clear and concrete. Vague definitions that don't include precise descriptions of the responsibilities and expectations for the position can lead to bad hires.

For instance, if you are planning to expand your sales force, you might need to create a new sales management position to supervise and motivate the larger sales team. There are many different ways to construct an effective sales organization, some of which involve installing different tiers of people best suited for the complexity of the type of clients they will sell to. Have you considered this stratification of your sales organization as you developed your criteria? The goals and responsibilities for each new position will need to reflect your specific expectations for the role and for sales growth from that role.

Once you have created a detailed job description, the next step is to define the criteria you will use to sort through applicants for the position. These criteria need to reflect the specific qualities required to fill the position as described in the definition. I cannot emphasize enough the need to use both art and science when coming up with these criteria. Remember to spend time analyzing the qualities that the successful candidate will need. Be sure to prioritize these qualities from most important to least important.

One essential tool is a data-driven assessment of the best people in your organization who have performed well in the same or similar positions. There are a variety of online assessments available, and I suggest picking one that works well for the roles you are hiring for. I would also suggest using an expert to help you calibrate the tool to your specific company, culture, and role if you want the output from the assessment to be useful and valid. Even if it is an entirely new position, this assessment informed by your intuitive knowledge of your expectations, the organization and its culture, and similar positions advertised in your industry will contribute to making the list of criteria as effective as possible. Involve your senior managers, especially those to whom the new hire will report. Their insights will be invaluable as well. Remember, if you cannot define the concrete criteria for a successful hire with specificity, the process will break down at this initial stage. For example, when looking for a sales leader, there are very specific requirements necessary in any sales management role, including the following:

- demonstrated success in sales management
- demonstrated success in solution selling

- demonstrated success as prudent business manager, who understands the need for some risk and proactive investment in the business, i.e., someone who thinks in terms of results and long-term strategy
- demonstrated facility and skill in setting direction and vision as well as in "rolling up the sleeves" and working in day-to-day tactical sales activities
- demonstrated leadership capacity with excellent communication and listening skills and ability to work exceptionally well in a collaborative environment
- demonstrated strong cognitive ability and intellectual curiosity
- demonstrated success as motivator, coach, and trainer
- demonstrated success as strategic thinker, yet comfortable to do the day-to-day work
- demonstrated success as a proactive change agent
- demonstrated ability to influence and persuade others
- demonstrated excellent questioning, listening, negotiating, qualifying, and closing skills
- demonstrated results in disciplined pipeline management

The basic criteria for selecting the best candidates often include: skills, experience, soft and hard competencies, credentials, reputation, and flexibility concerning travel. There may be others more specific to the position itself.

For example, the criteria necessary for hiring a relationship development salesperson in a company expanding from start-up to a second-stage business are dramatically different from those used in a company like Procter & Gamble for the same position. In larger, established companies, the principal hiring criteria might support maintaining the existing relationships of long-time clients rather than the aggressive development of new clients. This category of candidate is known as "the farmer" who nurtures and keeps a client relationship fertile. Companies moving into the second-stage growth routinely look for "the prospector/hunter" category of candidate for this position; they need someone who has a demonstrated ability to find, secure, and develop new business.

When building a sales organization for a second-stage company, in addition to the typical language regarding actual prospecting, handling objections, selling, and closing skills, I added attributes that I found highly correlated with success in the role. While not a complete list, some of these attributes included the following:

- is career motivated, and he or she is willing to invest significant time and effort
- displays a high level of intellectual curiosity
- is socially bold
- shows ability to be an advocate for the client
- has demonstrated an ability to develop deep and lasting relationships across an organization
- shows well-developed communication skills, ability to discern unspoken politics, what is said and what remains unsaid, and the real motivations of the client

The above list certainly does not apply in all sales roles, but every environment has a set of attributes and competencies, in addition to the technical requirements for the role, that will correlate with success in that role. The important thing is to understand what they are and to have a process that brings to light evidence that the behaviors necessary for success are in fact an established part of the repertoire of the people you hire.

The execution of this first principle can be tedious. It is always tempting to skip this entire process on the theory that "I'll know talent when I see it." This haphazard approach invariably leads to wasted recruiting efforts and poor hires. Take the time at the front end to define the job and the criteria with sufficient rigor and discipline so that you'll be able to hire the right person.

While specific criteria are vital to hiring the best candidate, it is important to be flexible when assessing each candidate. For instance, cognitive ability as demonstrated by class standing in graduates of four-year colleges is a key criterion to success in almost any job. When hiring for more complex consultative sales roles, I have used the 50th percentile as the absolute minimum bar when hiring sales talent. I use a much higher bar when hiring for senior or executive level talent.

However, it is important to weigh cognitive ability against the ability to communicate effectively with colleagues, creativity, and a healthy emotional intelligence (EQ) is an important general criterion, but these other factors might be equally or more important for the specific position.

For most employers, relevant experience appears to be among the easiest criteria to list for candidates applying for positions other than entry level. Experience is easily quantifiable and concrete, but it can be dramatically overvalued in the hiring process. I encourage you to think about the nature and the depth of experience that are really needed for the position in question. Experience does not always convey the full picture of a person's potential and capabilities.

Assessing the value of experience is one aspect that involves the art of hiring smart. While it is good to include experience as one of the basic criteria for most positions, it needs to be put in the context of the candidate's other attributes. Adhering too closely to a specific type or level of experience can result in excluding candidates who may have far greater potential than the ones you end up considering because you defined your experience requirement in a very narrow fashion.

For example, a number of years back I was making a trip to support a new manager who was running our brand-new Los Angeles office.

The manager picked me up at the airport. In the car with her was the newly hired office administrator, a person the manager had worked with at another company in a similar administrative role. On the way back to the office, I started asking this new hire about her background. Since we were driving on the 405 Freeway in LA, we had some time. It turns out she was a USC graduate, did very well there, and appeared to have—on the surface—most of the criteria we were looking for to fill one of the business development positions in that office.

After consulting with the manager, we agreed to put her through the recruitment and assessment process we used at the time for business development positions. She profiled beautifully. Shortly after that, we offered her the position and started the search for a new office administrator. She went on to rank in the top tier of successful business development professionals in the company.

If we had been limited by our requirement that any candidate for a business development role needed a minimum of three to five years of successful consultative sales experience, this person never would have been considered for a role she was ideally suited for.

PRINCIPLE TWO: PROCESS AND DISCIPLINE

As companies grow into and beyond their second stage of growth, some sort of formalized recruitment process must be put in place. Once you follow the first principle and define the job and the criteria necessary for the successful candidate, creating a system that will effectively find, interview, and vet potential candidates is the next important step in hiring top-tier talent. However, you must have the discipline to follow the process.

I realized how important process and discipline are early in my career. Coming off a successful eight-year tenure at General Electric during which I had to hire a number of people, I thought I was "pretty good" at recruiting talent because many of the individuals I had hired were quite good. However, I now was in an entrepreneurial environment, without the GE brand, with the need to build teams quickly and from the ground up. At the end my first year, my hit rate of high-quality hires was at best 50 percent. While this might be acceptable in a huge corporation like General Electric and when you are only adding incrementally to the team each year, it is a huge problem in a second-stage business when entire teams are new.

Under pressure to get the offices up and running in a big hurry, I hired the wrong people to manage each of the three California locations all in the same year. Since it is highly unlikely that B-level managers can hire A-level teams, the ineffectiveness of these managers affected the entire network, and none of the offices were performing close to expectations. After a particularly memorable board meeting where the chairman of the board mentioned "it might be a good idea to go California and not come back until the problem was fixed," I came to the realization that I had to change the hiring process—and fast.

To fix the problem, I ended up engaging an industrial/organizational psychologist. The goal was twofold: to fix the problems that I had created in California and to put in place the process and discipline for future recruitment efforts that ultimately would mitigate the risk of this type of disaster happening again. This individual helped me institute a new recruitment process that would improve the success rate of hiring for the high-value, high-risk, field roles of branch general manager and account manager—the leaders of the marketing and the business development teams in each office.

We developed the following procedure for all candidates:

- a set of standardized assessment tests for all candidates; this included a list of the most critical and necessary competencies and behaviors that correlated with success in the role
- a fact-based profile for candidates, based on the assessment of the entire team of managers and salespeople to correlate specific test scores with high performance

- an interview guide for each position and a scoring sheet for the answers to the questions

This procedure was designed to stand the test of time and ensure compliance. We trained all of our hiring managers in using this procedure. No one could be hired without going through it. No exceptions. The results for each candidate were quantified and reviewed with the appropriate decision makers. They served as the objective basis for all hiring decisions.

Within one year of instituting this process, sales turnover in the company was reduced to less than 10 percent, and performance grew exponentially. The company ended up growing organically from $3 million in 1989 to a run rate of over $100 million in 1994, culminating in a public offering in May 1994, which turned out to be the second-best IPO on NASDAQ in that year. If I had had the foresight to institute this system a year earlier, I estimate that company would have grown even faster with a run rate of $150 million.

PRINCIPLE THREE: DON'T SETTLE FOR MEDIOCRITY

Even when a formal process is in place and the hiring managers are trained to follow it, there is usually pressure to hire the best *available* candidate and move on. This is especially true when you're pushing to meet your second-stage expansion goals. What do you do when the candidates are acceptable but not stellar? Mediocre, but not special? It's a tricky question and requires good judgment and wisdom.

Although it's hard to believe, studies have shown that the cost associated with hiring the wrong person is far greater than the cost of leaving an existing position unfilled. The wrong person can damage your brand and client relationships, disrupt in-house staff, and drain resources without contributing to growth. Resist the temptation to hire someone just to have a "warm body" in place. It will save you headaches and money.

There is no hard-and-fast rule of thumb, but if the decision is difficult, or if no one is enthusiastic about the candidate, you are likely making a mistake if you press ahead. If there is serious debate among the team members about a candidate, this usually means that the person will not work out well in the long run. You are far better off passing on this person and continuing the search for a better candidate.

This is where most of the mistakes are made in the hiring process. Open headcount, pressure to fill jobs, a belief that we are sufficiently skilled at managing so that we can remedy "or work with" the candidates' known weaknesses—all this causes us to lower our standards and hire individuals we should not hire. If you are making excuses, shrugging your shoulders as if to say "it's worth a shot" or just plain want to get it over with, you will likely be making a mistake. When doing this, ask yourself if you would be willing to bet $1 million of your own money that this person will work out. If you hesitate, don't settle. Keep interviewing.

In some companies, effective recruiting requires establishment of a process that is a bit different. However, a different process does not necessarily mean the process is without discipline and rigor. If you think about SoulCycle, which we introduced in the previous chapter, one of the fundamental leverage points to its success is the quality of its instructors. After all, if someone is paying a premium price to have an exercise experience, much of the quality of that experience will depend on the skill and personality of the instructor. These instructors have to be *really* good. In many ways, the instructor is the product SoulCycle is selling. Thus, in the case of SoulCycle, the hiring process is more of an audition than an interview. It is, in many ways, like selecting an actor for a part. In reality, an instructor must also be an entertainer, and this latter capability matters more than the technical skills.

With this understanding then, it is not surprising that SoulCycle hires not for experience but for capability; the managers are looking for performers, not accomplished bike racers. According to *New York* magazine, a typical selection process will begin with 80 or so people who audition to become an instructor. The managers select eight to twelve to go through the eight-week training period, and perhaps seven of these will make the final cut. The applicants are not paid for this training period, but the "classes" are free. A different approach in some ways, but the idea at its core is the same as in the above-described process. SoulCycle understands what competencies correlate with the success of instructors, and they have built a hiring process to ensure that they hire the people who will be "A" players. If you think about it, this eight-week process will thoroughly vet every candidate, and hiring mistakes will be very rare. On the company's web site, the instructors occupy a very prominent place. When you look at the physical beauty and near-perfect conditioning of each of these people along with their entertainer qualities, you will understand why.

PRINCIPLE FOUR: ALWAYS BE RECRUITING

Professional salespeople have a saying: "Always be selling." As you move forward with your second-stage growth plan, priorities and personnel will change. So, as leader in the march forward, you should have a similar motto: "Always be recruiting." Good people can come from any number of sources, and you need to remain vigilant to find talent. True top-tier talent is rare; you have to be searching for it all the time.

Despite the current trend to rely on the power of websites, LinkedIn, and other social networking sites, a personal referral from someone you trust and respect is still one of the best ways to find new talent. Some of the best people come as referrals from other high performers already in your company. Be proactive in leveraging this source. Be willing to take the time to meet with people even when you have no idea if they fit into your current needs. Referrals from other professionals in your industry or related fields are also a great resource. One of the biggest obstacles affecting recruiting effectiveness is the hiring manager's inability to build a sufficiently large pool of candidates so that there is a sufficient number of top-tier candidates to consider. Take the time to do this yourself, or hire the resources to do this for you, but be sure you build a large pool of potential candidates before you decide to hire.

MBO Partners, a second-stage growth company based outside of Washington, D.C., adhered to this strategy as it grew. Gene Zaino, the CEO, has handpicked each of his direct reports over the past few years as he geared up for more rapid growth. In all cases, either he or someone he knew well had extensive experience with each candidate prior to that person joining the MBO Partners team.

In nearly every case, Gene met the person he ultimately hired well before his plan to expand was implemented. He made it his business to learn about the candidate's personality, cultural fit, capability, and potential before the person joined his team. He took the time to cultivate the relationship and vet the candidate over time against his criteria for the positions he would need to fill.

A number of years ago, Gene saw an opportunity to formally develop an entirely new channel for MBO's services that they had been servicing on an ad hoc basis up to that point. He was able to move quickly on this market opportunity as he had been building a relationship during the four years prior with an executive he believed would make an outstanding president of this new division. Once the opportunity presented itself, he contacted the candidate and put him through the hiring process. But to some extent, the hiring process had already been underway for four years. Gene's knowledge of this candidate's suitability served to expedite the process with a minimum of risk. Today, this channel, under the leadership of this smart hire, is an important contributor to MBO's overall success.

The overall benefit derived from a continuous recruitment philosophy is high even when you have modest growth aspirations. This is overwhelmingly true that when you are driving for aggressive growth as part of your second stage. Building a pipeline of great people your company can hire as the needs materialize—whether in six months or two years—is essential. Without a pool of talent to draw on quickly, you risk not optimizing your results as you scramble to find the talent to fill an immediate staffing need. Going to look for the talent only after you recognize the need will not stack the odds in your favor.

For example, as I mentioned earlier, one of the board members at Parson Group was a professor at the Harvard Business School. He would refer students to Parson Group who he thought were quality candidates for the company, which was then in a serious growth mode. Over a period of five years, we hired six of this professor's former students. One of these hires was right out of HBS, but the others had followed more traditional paths of taking jobs in consulting or in big consumer products companies after graduating from HBS. Somehow, our board member knew a few of his former students were unhappy in these large corporate roles and wanted something a bit more entrepreneurial. He would send these individuals to talk to me. In some cases, we had an immediate need, and we could hire the person as soon as he or she successfully completed our hiring process.

In most instances, however, we met with the person, learned about his or her talents and expectations, where the candidate wanted to live, and if the person seemed suitable, we would file the information away and consider that person for future employment. When a need of ours matched up with the candidate, and he or she was still interested and available, we would move the person into the hiring process. Certainly, this was not the only strategy we employed, as the firm ultimately grew to 600 people at all levels of experience. But it did produce some terrific results.

Not everyone loves sports analogies, but on the talent front we can all learn from how sports teams focus relentlessly on talent. They are always seeking individuals who can join the team and contribute. High-performing players make the difference between winning and losing. Players who don't contribute in the expected fashion are cut. I am not suggesting that you adopt the exact hiring practices of an NFL coach. However, it is clear to me that when the opportunity of adding top-tier people to your team presents itself, you need to recruit them as seriously as the coaches recruit players.

PARTING WORDS

When your company is poised to jump into second-stage growth, smart hires give you a competitive advantage. Talented people at all levels of your company will exceed your expectations; mediocre people will drag your company down. There is a profound difference in the results produced by an average person compared to those of one who is exceptional. In order to recruit top talent, you need to have the insight and discipline to evaluate candidates thoroughly. Haphazard hiring practices, inconsistency, and lack of discipline will produce disastrous results. The evidence shows that it costs far more to hire badly than not to hire at all.

Despite the pressure to expand, you need to take the time to hire smart. Define the job and its criteria clearly and concretely. Institute a formal evaluation process for soliciting candidates and evaluate them objectively and in interviews. Train hiring managers to have the discipline to follow the process without exception. Remain open and flexible to factors that affect the stated criteria, such as experience and skills. Despite the pressure to hire, don't settle for the mediocre or the expedient candidate. And regardless of your hiring needs, always be recruiting top people. Create a pool of top-tier candidates that you can rely on when the time is right.

Your organization is only as strong as its people. As much as you'd like to do everything yourself, as a second-stage entrepreneur, you need to delegate the responsibility for growth to a talented team of professionals. As you build your business and gear up for strong growth, a relentless focus on getting your hiring strategy right is the surest way to achieve your goals.

Chapter 6

THE NEW MODEL FOR SELLING

SECOND-STAGE ENTREPRENEURSHIP IS THE moment of truth. This is the stage where your company grows up. You are no longer sitting in your house or garage or in an open space with rented desks shouting to your coworkers about ideas that will move the business forward. It is time to think less about survival and more about growth.

You've proven that your start-up is successful. You've created a game plan for your second-stage growth. Your products are innovative and competitive. You've got capital resources and a board of experienced advisors. You're hiring the best and brightest. But unless your company is built on a business model that depends on marketing to drive volume, such as traditional retail, Internet-driven, or business-to-consumer, you probably rely on a dedicated sales organization to get and maintain new clients. Second-stage growth requires you to reevaluate your current sales team to meet the company's new goals and demands.

For example, consider a company called WebFilings. WebFilings was started in 2008 to address a specific need in the financial reporting market. The founders knew that new regulations would require all public companies to file quarterly and annual statements with the SEC in XBRL format in 2009. The business plan of the company was to build a cloud-based software technology platform that would assist in the automation of filing these reports electronically to help public companies to be in compliance with the SEC's regulations.

Working as quickly as they could, the founders successfully launched the beta version of the software in 2009. Then, WebFilings had to figure out how to drive rapid revenue growth to seize the market opportunity ahead of potential competitors. The company had to find a way to prospect, qualify, and engage potential customers for the WebFilings software. This was a massive task considering that

WebFilings' prospects included all public companies in the United States, a total of approximately 15,000 at the time.

WebFilings was faced with a classic problem for start-up companies that sell enterprise software: how to penetrate a significant percentage of the available market as quickly and thoroughly as possible. They had created an entirely new product ahead of the competition. The market was about to explode. The WebFilings business plan included the creation of a highly effective sales organization as a critically important component of the initial launch. WebFilings set out to hire professional salespeople fitting the classic "hunter" profile because it believed they could be successful selling reasonably high volumes of relatively low-ticket ($25,000 to $50,000 average cost per year) software licenses. The company needed salespeople who could hit the ground running and make an immediate impact.

The sale of enterprise software is a classic transaction sale and is not typically relationship-based. The sales process was straightforward: get interest, get a meeting, show the benefits of the software, handle objections, close, and move on. In this fast-moving market, if a prospect does not show interest, move on to the next one. After a sale, a different group within the company typically handles implementation and ongoing support. This keeps the salespeople focused on what they do best: selling. Delivery and support would become someone else's concern.

In the case of WebFilings, the management team had previous experience in the software industry and knew what it took to get a fast-paced software company going. The managers knew the kind of experience and skill set needed to ramp up a software sales force quickly and effectively. WebFilings would provide the necessary training in their product, but the learning curve could not be steep. There simply wasn't enough time. They targeted candidates who already knew about software sales. Motivated by a unique product, a huge potential base of well-financed clients, and a lucrative sales incentive, WebFilings could hire strong candidates and manage the team tightly to metrics.

Since 2009, the company has been extremely aggressive in the hiring of software sales professionals. Their current sales force now numbers nearly 100 professionals. Thanks to their efforts, the revenues have grown from zero in 2009 to $700,000 in 2010 and to $15 million in 2011 to over $50 million in 2012. They are highly likely to exceed the $100 million revenue threshold in 2013. In this short period of time, they can already claim over 50 percent of the Fortune 500 companies as clients. Yes, the company has a compelling product. Yes, market timing was perfect. However, in order to grow, in order to create value for the investors and management team, the founders knew that a substantial investment in a sales organization was necessary to take full advantage of the market opportunity.[1]

However, not every second-stage company has the financial capital for building a sales team as aggressively as WebFilings—or needs to do so. For example, consider the experience of a company called Brandtrust. Brandtrust was founded 15 years ago by Daryl Travis. Travis had previously worked for a global advertising agency. He wanted to create a different business model by offering clients services not available from the big firms. Through research that revealed deep and hidden insights into clients' individual brands and customers of their brands, Brandtrust's highly collaborative, discovery-driven approach helped clients solve complex innovation and brand issues.

Brandtrust built slowly and steadily over the first 10 years. It got to the point where the business model was proven, the company was solid, but new business development was limited by the amount of time Travis and a few other key members of his senior team could spend on prospecting for new clients. Not coming from the world of sales, his initial idea of scaling up sales was to set up more meetings with prospective new clients. So his solution to the dilemma was to outsource the function of generating leads to a firm specializing in setting appointments. This firm was hired to make phone calls to set up meetings either for Travis or for someone else on the senior team.

This approach worked well, and Travis saw the benefit that came from having people committed to a business development function without the distraction of also having to serve clients and bill hours. The success of the appointment setting team made him realize he had to expand the in-house business development function to a dedicated sales team consisting of a sales manager, four outbound appointment setters, and a team of sales professionals. The company implemented a CRM system, has a defined sales process, and has enjoyed double-digit growth in each of the years since this strategy was implemented.[2]

However, as Travis learned, simply broadening your exposure to new clients is not enough to reach accelerated growth. You need a sales team that is trained to optimize prospects. The key factor in sales success is instituting a defined sales process and training the sales team to follow through with discipline, insight, and ingenuity.

Many books have been written on a variety of selling models and sales success. This book cannot possibly do justice to this entire topic by giving an overview of the most effective approaches. Rather, I have included a few basic ideas I have implemented in three successive start-ups with great success each time. These ideas are intended to augment your sales strategy. They are:

- develop a "power pitch"
- create a defined sales process
- emphasize the value of being a client's trusted advisor
- develop stories that illustrate the value of your product or service

THE POWER PITCH

Research has proven that a sales person has less than one minute to engage a client. If not engaged within that short time, the client "zones" out, and the probability of progressing in the sales cycle diminishes substantially. The presence and personality of the salesperson certainly plays a role in the client's initial reaction. More important, though, is what the salesperson first says to a potential client. Often referred to as "an elevator pitch," this is a vital tool for sales success. This seems like a very basic sales concept, but it is more difficult than it appears to train sales people to deliver this pitch effectively.

To evaluate your team's ability to deliver this pitch, I suggest a very simple test. Ask five business development people in your firm to state, in thirty seconds or less, *what your firm does*. Then ask five individuals in other parts of the firm who are not involved in sales. Finally, ask five trusted customers or clients the same question. I think you will be amazed, perhaps even alarmed, at what you hear.

The power pitch must state what your makes your company unique in a clear and compelling fashion. The specific content of the pitch will change depending on the situation or role of the client being pitched, but the basic message needs to be *targeted and consistent* to be effective. For instance, if you're pitching a CFO you might use technical or financial industry jargon. However, when pitching a midlevel manager or decision maker, less technical business oriented language might be more effective. Part of the skill of delivering an effective power pitch comes from knowing how best to approach your audience.

The importance of the power pitch cannot be overstated. If you can get every person in your company to know and use this pitch regardless of the individual's role, you will automatically set yourself up to perform better than your competitors who don't take that step. The challenge is that it is not easy to get your employees to take this seemingly "simple" task seriously. Everyone thinks that he or she is smart enough to wing it, especially sales people, and the results are often ineffective, haphazard, and inaccurate delivery of the pitch.

I have found that the only way to get people to learn both the message and its importance is to host a session designed to address the basic points of an effective power pitch. Whether you do it through virtual conferencing or have small groups meet face-to-face, this approach will strengthen your entire team's concept of how to craft a strong pitch. The basic points include:

- What are the points of interest?
- What are the differentiators?
- What are the proof points?
- How to tailor the pitch to different classes of clients

Once there is a general consensus on the critical talking points for the pitch, each participant needs to recite his or her version of the pitch in front of a video recorder. This exercise is time consuming but well worth the effort. Seeing themselves on a screen, as painful as this can sometimes be, is the only way to get the team members to recognize the importance of refining and practicing the pitch. Once they fully understand the need for a tight, consistent, and well-delivered pitch, their sales performance will increase markedly.

I recently conducted a training class for a very successful private equity-backed health care services firm based in Los Angeles. The goal was to teach a team of 20 outbound telemarketers how to be more effective in setting appointments at the company's facilities around the country. We started the day putting together the basic script as I suggested above and then moved into a session on how to best handle objections. Most thought the exercise was not at all difficult—until it came time to incorporate what they had learned and actually perform a live role play in front of the camera. Not surprisingly, the gap between how good the participants thought they were at doing this versus what they each observed while watching the recorded performance became the catalyst for the team to practice and work at building this important skill.

A DEFINED SALES PROCESS

The next idea to consider when training your sales team is to make sure that you establish a defined sales process. Nearly every larger company has a defined sales process, but for entrepreneurial companies and for those just entering the second stage of growth this is not the norm. Again, this is another fairly basic concept, but requires some detailed planning of the specific steps necessary to bring a sales opportunity from finding the prospect to a closed deal. Every person on the team needs to follow the same sales process for the entire sales effort to be effective.

Selling anything to anyone is one of the most difficult roles in any company. From a management standpoint, it certainly does not help that many of the best salespeople work on a highly idiosyncratic model that they carefully protect for fear of competition from their associates. This engrained habit is hard to break. However, sharing best practices with the team will elevate the performance of each person on the team and needs to be a goal in creating a defined sales process accessible to everyone. This is particularly important in training new salespeople.

A well-conceived sales process breaks the entire sales cycle into discreet but connected steps. Building the procedure on reaching certain milestones to move it forward helps in mapping the clear path to closing the sale. The process needs to be concrete and logical, based on a clear quid-pro-quo equation: follow the steps and the probability of a successful transaction is greatly increased. While each situation is different, and the human factor often necessitates some adjustments, starting out with a defined sales process for your sales team gives each member a roadmap to follow toward a successful conclusion.

Installing a defined sales process puts discipline into what might otherwise be a totally reactive and inconsistently executed activity. It also requires a discussion of where to apply resources, which opportunities are worth pursuing, and which should be left for someone else to chase.

Most sales processes share some basic attributes, which are listed below. Depending on your company structure, your industry, and your plan for growth, you may need to modify some points, jettison others, and perhaps create entirely new ones. But the points listed here serve as a practical foundation for any defined sales process. A version of this sales process has worked well for me in four different companies.

STEP 1: ACCOUNT RESEARCH AND PREPARATION

- **Stage 1**: 0% Account research and preparation

STEP 2: IDENTIFYING

- **Stage 2**: 1% Prospecting a new opportunity
- **Stage 3**: 5% Initial call. The contact has been called. Minimal information has been gathered. Initial capabilities presented.

STEP 3: QUALIFYING

- **Stage 4**: 10% Opportunity profiled / qualified. Prospect appears to be serious, and there is a potential fit. Business and performance issues identified.
- **Stage 5**: 15% Assessment. In-depth assessment of prospect's business. Client or prospect has the budget to implement a solution. Have a plan on how to calculate ROI.

STEP 4: DEVELOPING THE RELATIONSHIP

- **Stage 6**: 25% Consult. A solution has been developed; a presentation, proposal, and pricing have been generated, approved by the managing director, and presented to the prospect.
- **Stage 7**: 35% Short list. We have confirmed we are on the short list. This list typically includes no more than two other competitors.
- **Stage 8**: 40% Corporate visit. We have met the CEO/C-level executives and have presented our proposed solution. Visited with client leaders at their offices or ours.
- **Stage 9**: 50% Met decision maker—favorable. We have met the decision maker and believe he or she favors our solution.

STEP 5: CLOSING

- **Stage 10**: 60% We are the selected vendor. We have been told we are the selected solution provider.
- **Stage 11**: 70% Negotiation. The prospect is negotiating on price and/or terms. Contract delivered to prospect for review.

- **Stage12**: 80% Contract terms agreed. Pricing and terms have been agreed and approved by us and by client.
- **Stage 13**: 90% Pending signature. Waiting for client or prospect to sign agreement.
- **Stage 14**: 100% Signed agreement.

STEP 6: EXPANSION

Energizing your sales professionals with a company-wide process will help the entire team optimize its efforts and push forward to greater and more cost-effective performance. However, there is no need to recreate the wheel. As I mentioned earlier, there are already dozens of established sales processes you can choose from. Most that I have seen look very similar; they are tailored to the complexity of the product or service sold and likely differ depending on whether the sale involves an individual buyer or a more complicated enterprise with many buyers and potentially an equal number of influencers. Nearly all of the sales training and development companies, in addition to having a library of skills courses that they offer, also have defined sales processes they encourage their clients to implement in addition to the training. While the exact sales process decision is an important one, what matters more is the emphasis on discipline: everyone must follow the process.

One very important consideration when establishing a sales process is establishing the gates that govern moving from one stage to another. For example, it is not uncommon in the sales processes I have overseen to dictate that for a particular opportunity to move out of the "developing" phase into the "closing" phase, there must be a client representative acting as an advocate for your company. Another common gate might be that a contract must be signed in order for an opportunity to move from "closing" to "implementing." This perhaps sounds a bit too detailed, but remember that probability factors depend in part on where an opportunity stands in the process, so inaccuracy and inconsistency in correctly defining the stage of an opportunity will overstate or understate the probability of a deal closing, leading to inaccurate revenue forecasts.

THE VALUE OF BEING A CLIENT'S TRUSTED ADVISOR

In *The Challenger Sale: Taking Control of the Customer Sale* that I mentioned in chapter 5, the authors make the point that the world of the traditional sales model has changed forever.[3] Today, customers are in a position to learn quite a bit about your company before they ever meet with a sales representative. With some potential buyers, there is no longer the need for a preamble about who your company is or what it does. The client most likely will know quite a bit about your firm after the initial contact. As a result, the sales professional needs to work with the client in a fashion quite different from what many have done previously.

Based upon timely research data, the authors suggest that success in today's world of sales comes from a new model of selling. The methodology they suggest is that salespeople talk less about their company's product or service and more about the client's needs and educating the customer about how best to resolve them. In sum, the salesperson works toward achieving the status of a trusted advisor to the client, not just that of a service provider.[4]

However, my personal view is that this concept, while certainly timely, is not at all new. It is a time-honored fact that a successful sales person has to figure out how to tilt the field in his or her direction to get the sale. The most effective strategy has always been to establish a sufficiently deep relationship with someone (or a number of people) in the client organization such that the salesperson can develop a level of understanding of the client's organization and business issues that is unique and superior to that of potential competitors. Once he or she is in the position of a valued advisor looking out for the client's best interests, the salesperson is in an excellent position to leverage that influence to get new business.

The key to all this is to execute the sales process in a fashion that allows you to help clients understand certain things they did not necessarily know about the market or industry. You help them analyze a situation in such a way that they come away with a different perspective than what they would otherwise have brought to the table. By doing this, you create a "need" that only your company is qualified to meet.

Thus the opportunity becomes what is known as a "sole-sourced" one. You don't have to fight off other vendors with competitive approaches, and while I am in no way suggesting that charging anything other than a fair price is ever smart, you will have some price flexibility if your solution is truly unique and the client perceives that your solution is uniquely positioned to offer the best path forward.

At Parson Group, we illustrated this powerful sales model to our sales team using the graphics, such as figures 6.1 and 6.2. Teaching our salespeople how to connect with a client as an advisor put them in a position to help their client with a solution to an issue the client may not have been aware of before. Nurturing this relationship, we ended up selling a large number of "customized" or "unique" services that had a big impact on driving our growth. Of course, it is not possible to have every sale come from a strong relationship as valued advisor to the client, but an effective sales team will use such relationships to best effect.

Figure 6.1   Selling strategies hierarchy

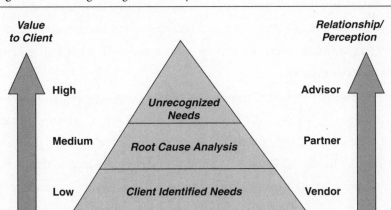

Figure 6.2   Selling strategies approach summaries

	"Identified" Needs	*"Root-Cause" Needs*	*"Unrecognized" Needs*
Who Identified Need?	Client	Client	Parson Group
Who Identified Solution?	Client	Parson Group	Parson Group
Type of Approach?	Reactive/Pull	Consultative/Push	Solution/Position
Client Perception of Parson Group?	Vendor	Partner	Advisor
Pricing Flexibility?	Low	Medium	High
Value to Client?	Low	Medium	High

THE VALUE OF STORIES

Think about all the speeches that you have heard over the years. Think about the reunions or family gatherings you have attended. Think about the companies that have achieved cultlike following? What do they all have in common? They all have stories, anecdotes about key events or successes. We are drawn to narratives, especially those that leave us with an insight or lesson. The more accessible and relevant the story is, the more we will remember not only the lesson but the storyteller as well.

Second-stage entrepreneurship builds on the story of the success of a start-up, the commitment to create new products and the rapid expansion of the organization and its facilities and resources. Clients are drawn to a winner, and stories communicate that better than any pie chart or growth chart.

For example, when you look at any company website, you'll note that there is a tab for "Our History" or "Who We Are" where you can read the story of the company. These stories serve a variety of purposes for the client. For new companies, they put a face to the company name by naming and picturing the founders. In nearly every case, they promote their growth, their sales concepts, and dedication to a unique or effective customer experience. They serve as a way for clients to learn about a company before they even think about doing business with it.

While these text-driven stories are the initial building blocks for a company's profile, the power of spoken stories is equally if not more important to the professional salesperson. As he or she builds a relationship with the client, the use of stories that illustrate the value of the company's products or services brings the client closer to wanting to acquire them. Stories also serve to demonstrate how the individual salesperson as a representative of the company has found solutions to the challenges encountered with other clients. Stories are one of the most dramatic tools for sales professionals to promote their company and garner new business.

However, not everyone is a great storyteller. It is difficult to develop a power pitch for most people without some coaching, and the same holds true for creating a collection of illustrative stories to share with clients. How do you make this an integral part of your selling model? How can all employees tell the stories that will promote the company to new customers and lead to growth?

First, you need to isolate the kinds of stories that will be attractive. Is the founding story of your company colorful and dramatic enough to illustrate the creativity and drive your company can offer to the client? What elements make it unique and compelling? Does the story of your success and subsequent commitment to second-stage growth showcase your growing market profile in your industry? Is the story of how your signature product or service was created and promoted exciting?

To begin the process of assembling these narratives, management needs to lead by staging informal meetings for sharing experiences that could be developed into stories. You need make sure that everyone knows the founding story, preferably from the founder himself or herself. Old photos, product demos, successful launches, and other aspects of the origin of the company help create the overall narrative.

Updating the company's story to include awards and spectacular growth elements, such as a new head office or expansion in all fifty states, is another aspect of the corporate story.

Even more important to the sales process are stories from customers or clients. Every client organization thinks that its business issues are unique. The savvy salesperson will use clients' willingness to share their own challenges and successes to cement their relationship and learn how best to meet their needs. It is important to train your salespeople to note that while clients perceive themselves as having their special set of challenges, there are always aspects of their experiences that are similar to what other clients have encountered. The truth is that many businesses have very similar issues.

It is very difficult to take a client on the same journey of establishing credibility and trust when using a narrative that is based more on features/benefits and does not include a story of some sort. If the salesperson is unsuccessful in establishing credibility and trust from the outset of the working relationship, a negative perception will develop, and the sales process will stall. And because this is a perception and thus subjective and not based on facts, the client will not feel comfortable sharing the specific reasons for being reticent with the salesperson. The sales person will not know what happened, only that the deal died. It is important to teach your people to be keenly aware of and measure "negative perceptions" and how to use stories to help turn those into positive perceptions.

While this process is really not overly complicated, getting to a point of proficiency in telling stories that are impactful takes real effort and skill. Each salesperson should become intimately familiar with a manageable number of specific stories about your company and its clients' experiences. Each of these stories is written up as a case study following a specific format meant to be shared with the entire team. But the stories are most effective when delivered as if they are impromptu narratives by the salesperson, totally customized to show similarities to the opportunity with a particular client or prospect. The stories only work if the salesperson has practiced telling them and has committed the main points of the stories to memory.

The most effective stories usually include some combination of the following qualities:

- the issue encountered by a client, specified by name
- how the client tried to resolve the issue without success
- how your company came up with a successful solution
- the ongoing success with that client

The best salespeople develop a large treasure trove of stories to cover nearly any example that might come up during the sales cycle. Yes, client organizations can indeed be unique, and from time to time you will run into completely new situations for which there is no set applicable story to tell. However, as a trusted advisor, you will discover entirely new ways your organization can help a client in a way no one thought possible and build a story on that for future use.[5]

While Shiftgig is still a very young company, it has already mastered a nice set of stories. The stories begin with the founder, Eddie Lou, being a recovering venture capitalist turned entrepreneur. The stories continue with the founder talking about the fact that he noticed that 18- to 23-year-olds were not on LinkedIn. Rather, they were on Facebook. Eddie Lou surmised that the reason that age group is not on LinkedIn is that people in this group don't have a career network. Thus, he correctly understood that neither Facebook nor LinkedIn offers a good solution to the service industry, which is a very large market that hires millions of people from this age group. As the company moved from product development to commercial launch, the stories were changed to users' actual experiences while using the platform. These stories are visible to Shiftgig users, they are featured in email marketing campaigns, and they highlight how individuals found a fantastic job. In other stories employers talk about how much better it is to hire using Shiftgig compared to previous methods. The stories must be working: less than a year after commercial launch, Shiftgig has more than a quarter million individual users and nearly ten thousand employers using the service.

In his book, *Let's Get Real or Let's Not Play* (Portfolio Hardcover, 2008), Mahan Kalsa stated that successful selling is really about helping clients be successful.[6] Stories help build credibility and trust and are a critical component in getting clients to open up and make their needs clear so that you can help them.

PARTING WORDS

As we've seen, second-stage entrepreneurship is about transforming the way you do business to achieve growth. In most cases, you'll need to reevaluate your present sales organization and your existing sales model to achieve this goal. In order to support sustained growth, you'll probably need to expand your sales team with talented and ambitious people dedicated to growing the company.

But hiring smart alone won't get you where you need to be. You'll need to institute a defined sales process and train the team to follow through with discipline. The process begins with the power pitch that will engage the client in the first contact. The sales process needs to underscore that the most effective model for selling is for each sales person to become more than a simple sales contact for goods and services. He or she needs to be trained in the process of becoming the client's trusted advisor who is there to help the client be successful by finding solutions to their challenges. An important tool in this process is the power of stories to cement and nurture this relationship with clients. This relationship is the driving principle for this new model of selling that will enable you to scale your company to second-stage growth and beyond.

Chapter 7

MANAGING BEYOND METRICS

SALES GROWTH IS VITAL for any company making the leap to second-stage growth. We've established the importance of hiring the best sales people, based on a combination of criteria including experience, talent, potential, and intelligence. With strong investment in a new and expanded sales force, the future is bright and your growth assured.

But if we examine the actual state of affairs of sales performance and first-level sales management over the past few years, a sobering picture emerges. Overall, the performance of sales organizations has not met expectations, and this has affected business growth.

For example, consider the following facts concerning sales organizations in the United States:

- Over the past two years, over 40 percent of salespeople did not achieve their annual quota (*CSO Insights 2011 and 2012*).[1]
- In 2010, sales organizations overall achieved less than 80 percent of their targets. Only 1 percent of firms said their forecast accuracy was better than 90 percent (*CSO Insights 2011 and 2012*).
- Sales organization turnover continues at 25 percent annually (*CSO Insights 2011 and 2012*).
- Of people new to a role, 46 percent fail within 18 months (*Chally Research*).[2]
- As many as 63 percent of Sales Executive Council members say their sales managers do not have the skills and competencies they need to *evolve* their sales model, and nearly 10 percent do not have the skills they need to be successful in the job today (*The Challenger Sale* 2011).[3]

This last bullet point is of considerable concern. Effective sales management is the "make or break" component of any sales initiative.

You could hire the best salespeople, have great products, and provide strong system support, but without decisive and innovative managers, the sales organization will not reach its full potential. Leaders are needed to develop and coach each salesperson, keep the team on message, spur growth efforts, and put fires out to keep any sales effort focused on meeting (or exceeding) goals.

The principal reason for poor sales performance usually can be traced to the first-level sales managers. This root cause is especially true in start-ups poised for second-stage growth. The company has new goals and needs to expand beyond its current client base. The sales skills that made the start-up successful enough to grow will not take it to the next level and beyond. Sales managers, to the extent they are on staff, are on the firing line. They need to buy into the new set of rules and expectations, implement changes, and manage the sales force to achieve success.

Most sales managers come from working in direct sales. In the majority of cases, it is their success in the field as sales professionals that got them promoted to management. At one level, this seems to makes sense. A top salesperson would naturally know what it takes to be successful in the field and be able to lead his or her colleagues to achieve that same success. However, experience tells us that this is not the case. The attributes that contribute to success in the field do not always translate to success in a sales manager role.

To use a sports analogy, promoting a top salesperson to sales manager is like taking a star running back and making him an offensive line coach.

He might be good or even great in his current role as a star running back. However, his talents on the playing field, his instinct, ferocity, endurance, stamina, and speed are not relevant to the talents required by a coach. As an athlete, while he might be a team player, he is single-minded, focused on his specific role, and not all that concerned about how his fellow teammates perform theirs (notwithstanding his blockers).

A coach has to take the larger view of the team and the game itself. He needs to take into consideration the strengths and weaknesses of each player. He needs to make sure the players understand and adhere to the plays. He needs to be flexible in the face of competition, change gears when necessary, communicate the changes quickly and clearly, and then lead the team to victory. His individual strengths as a player don't count anymore. His focus must be on the team.

Any business poised for second-stage growth can't afford to make this mistake of hiring a player who is not well suited to being a coach. Businesses in that stage need their star salespeople in the field to continue the sales momentum that helped make the start-up a success. The practice of promoting highly effective salespeople to sales management positions without considering the critical requirements for the role could account for the high percentage of managers coming to the job without the core skills and competencies to be successful at it. This statistic, coupled with the equally alarming fact that nearly half of all people hired to perform a role new to them fail within the first year and half, indicates that there needs to be a better way to bolster first-level sales management.

Let's think about this in a different way—what is the primary focus of a salesperson? Typically, salespeople are trying to generate as much revenue as possible by selling the products and services in their portfolio. They gauge their success primarily by their position in internal rankings regarding revenue and monthly closings compared to that of their peers, and they want to be certain they qualify for the company sales incentive trip.

So, imagine the culture shock when the individual salesperson moves to a role in sales management. Rather than being a solo flyer, he or she is suddenly responsible for the careers, successes, struggles, revenue, and profit margins of the others on the team. It takes a person well suited to, willing, and committed to take on this responsibility and make this adjustment.

DEFINING A SALES MANAGER

As your company enters its second stage, it is unlikely that you will have the ability to promote someone from within to the role of sales manager. If somehow you have the depth and skill on your team to pull this off, that is great, but most companies are not sufficiently well developed to accomplish this until they are a few years into the second stage of growth. That means you will be required to find the talent you need from outside your company. The same principles we talked about in the previous chapter apply. Determine what you need and then hire carefully.

Start with the first rule of hiring smart: the job description. While the role of sales manager may vary depending on the size and core structure of the organization, there are several key responsibilities that are shared; these include the following:

- recruiting, hiring, and firing staff
- onboarding and training
- setting the local sales plan to be consistent with the business strategy
- creating and managing budgets
- establishing the local sales culture to be consistent with the company values
- strategizing the pursuit of large opportunities and key client relationships
- mentoring, coaching, and supervising the sales team
- troubleshooting problems
- innovating existing systems to respond to shifting marketplace
- monitoring sales goals for the team and the individual salespeople
- establishing and nurturing the local sales culture

How many of these responsibilities reflect the skills gained in the field while working as an individual contributor salesperson? The answer is very few. As I mentioned earlier, the qualities that make a successful salesperson don't necessarily make an effective sales manager. Strong sales experience, while a critical part of overall profile of a qualified candidate, should not be the deciding factor in either hiring an outside candidate or promoting a candidate from inside the organization.

I am not suggesting that you steer away from successful sales people when you are looking for managers. On the contrary, success in a direct selling role is one of the critical prerequisites for success in a sales management role. It is critical that the sales leader knows how to sell. But he or she must also know how to select talent and must master the other skills of effective leadership and management. A promotion to sales manager is clearly a reward for outstanding sales performance over some extended period of time. It also serves to keep top producers with the company instead of having them leave for opportunities elsewhere. If the candidate shows ambition and a willingness to learn, the right management training program could result in a superlative manager.

THE FOUNDER AS SALES MANAGER

In a second-stage company, building the sales organization is especially tricky. Often, the founder or CEO becomes the de facto sales manager. This is often done to save the expense of hiring a dedicated sales manager. However, this approach is shortsighted. If your second-stage business plan calls for the expansion of your sales team, the cost of a sales manager to guide that team needs to be part of the investment as well.

Sometimes, founders think that they are the person best suited for the role. If the founder is not a trained sales manager, as is often the case, this approach is highly unlikely to work. It is analogous to the idea of having someone with no formal training in finance or accounting in the role of controller or CFO. But because managing a team of sales professionals sounds nontechnical and does not require a specific college degree, many arrive at the conclusion that they certainly can fill that role. After all, how hard can it be?

Even if the founder has great personal sales skills and has been trained and has experience in sales management, it is unlikely that this approach will succeed for any sustained period of time. Sales management is a complex, full-time job. The job is to make the sales team successful. The CEO/founder will not have the time to perform this function successfully. There are just too many demands on his or her time to make this feasible.

Daryl Travis of Brandtrust (see chapter 5) is a great example of the short-lived success of this approach. He certainly knew how to sell quite effectively and took on this role from the beginning to generate business. However, as the company grew to the second stage, he could not devote enough time to selling. He was both serving clients and running the company. His senior management was also stretched too thin to give selling the attention it needed. So, he decided to go outside the company and recruited an individual specifically to build and manage the sales team.

As Travis learned, being an effective sales manager is a not simple task. It requires experience, training, and the requisite behavioral competencies to be successful in the role. It pays to invest by hiring a very talented person to run your sales organization, as this is your primary path to rapid growth.

THE SELLING MANAGER

Another approach that I have often seen in companies poised for second-stage growth is to hire a "selling manager." This person is expected to juggle managing the sales team with either maintaining relationships with a set of clients or working a territory. This practice is also not likely to work. It sets the manager up in competition with the team that he or she is intended to lead. It creates almost daily trade-offs in deciding whether the manager should spend time working with one of his or her own accounts or on managing the efforts of the team.

The idea of a selling manager sounds compelling. By giving the manager a territory or a number of reliable clients, the role becomes self-funding; this is an important point to consider when capital is tight. However, the investment deferred by having the leader in a combined role as both a producer and manager will be more than offset by his or her inability to properly support the sales team, and the team's performance will suffer as a result. For people in such a combined role, working with their own client tends to put more money in their pocket; spending time with the team tends to be better for the business overall. This is a trade-off to be avoided.

THE IMPORTANCE OF TRAINING

Billions of dollars are spent on training salespeople to be more effective in their job. Likewise, large companies spend billions investing in their senior leadership. The training program that was in place at GE when I joined that company is a perfect example.

When I was hired by GE straight out of college, I was put through a one-year training program as I began my sales career. After four years in a direct sales role, I knew I wanted to become a sales manager. However, the path to becoming a sales manager first required a stint in a staff role in headquarters, resulting in a move to Washington, D.C., and a role in sales support. After two years in this job supporting the sales organization on very large deals, I was fortunate enough to be provided the opportunity for a direct sales management role.

I had worked for five different sales managers during those four years in direct sales and for three additional managers during my time in a sales support capacity. As part of my staff role in major opportunity sales, I got to observe and know nearly every first-level and second-level field sales manager in the company. I had learned quite a bit about what to do—and about what not to do to motivate sales professionals. In addition to a variety of training programs for entry level roles, GE also had in place a very well regarded executive education facility in Crononville, New York. But even GE, a very large company with a huge commitment to training, did not have a specific training course for individuals entering a sales management role for the first time. The time in a staff role helped tremendously, but those of us who were placed into sales management roles for the first time afterward were somehow supposed to "figure this out on our own."

I was lucky; I had the benefit of second- and third-level managers who cared about my development and helped me learn what I needed to know to be an effective sales manager. I drew upon their experience and mentoring skills, which included daily conversations about what I should be doing to become an effective manager and leader. Some of this advice I solicited, and some was unsolicited but very much needed as I went through the normal learning curve of a role completely new to me.

While there's no substitute for this person-to-person attention, modern technology offers a wide array of training options for new managers. In addition to the traditional boots-on-the-ground scenario, new managers can take advantage of new data and reports from sophisticated CRM systems to help them supervise their sale steams. However, in smaller companies, many salespeople who are promoted simply see this as another step in their career and give little thought to how best to adapt and have even fewer resources to help them adapt to their new role.

EFFECTIVE SALES MANAGEMENT

Sales management is a balancing act, to be sure, and it is an admittedly difficult one. Superior sales managers understand that their primary job is to help their people be successful. The collective success of their team contributes to the manager's and the company's overall success. Yes, *management* matters, but coaching and development are the more important day-to-day responsibilities and should occupy the lion's share of the manager's time and effort. This concept and how to execute it is the most significant takeaway from any sales management training program.

How each salesperson does his or her job each day is what counts—the ability of the sales manager to assess and affect (through others) the quality of the interaction with customers and clients—this is what ultimately will characterize those who really are able to rise above the pack and deliver consistently strong performance. Somehow, somewhere along the way, this whole notion of coaching and development has been lost.

For many sales organizations, the role of the sales manager has been turned into one with the primary focus on metrics, based on analyzing reports coming from the CRM system that attempts to keep track of everything deemed to be important. Certainly, many of these metrics are very important. Weekly sales call activity will tend to correlate with results. Average deal size, total pipeline value, closing ratios, time in a phase of the sales process—all these metrics and others do matter. However, if managers are really going to be able to help their salespeople be successful, they need to spend time with them—on the ground, in planning sessions before sales calls, during sales calls, and in debriefing sessions after sales calls where plans are modified. Face-to-face, side-by-side.

Training is important, but it is through true coaching, guidance, and mentorship that what is learned during training sticks when needed most: in the office and in the field. Effective coaching is not a once-a-month activity or, as I have seen in some cases, a never-a-month activity.

A strong manager will work with every team member to establish appropriate goals. He or she will coach every team member when performance falls short to help the person understand what might be causing the shortfall, take corrective action, and then evaluate how the entire cycle is progressing. Then the process begins again. It is a constant, ongoing effort; it is a habit, not an event.

Over time, I have discovered a few basic steps that have helped me help sales managers become more effective.

INSIST ON A WRITTEN SALES PLAN

The rationale for the need to create an annual sales plan sounds fairly obvious. Yet, in my travels, I have found that even if in theory there is agreement that a written plan is a best practice and makes complete sense and that going through a planning process will lead to better results, the discipline in carrying out this practice varies widely. In some ways this is akin to the lack of discipline displayed in recruiting. Many second-stage companies have a very well developed strategic plan, but they have not yet embraced the power of a formal planning process at the operational and sales level.

The creation of a sales plan is a straightforward albeit time-consuming exercise. This process starts at the overall company level and then just cascades down through the rest of the organization. The hierarchy of planning activities is as follows:

1. Business planning
2. Territory planning
3. Account planning
4. Opportunity planning

Starting with business planning, the key is to understand what the overall objectives are that the sales unit must achieve. These are both financial and nonfinancial objectives. For example, what new products/services are we selling and at what level? What training do we need? What strategies and tactics must be implemented to reach the objectives? What direct and indirect sales channels make sense? Is there a logical partner strategy? How many and what type of sales resources are necessary to have adequate coverage to implement the plan? In simplistic terms, given the need to hit a certain revenue target, what must happen collectively with each member of the sales team, each client, each prospect, and each opportunity for the company to achieve its goal? A business plan is needed for the consolidated sales group overall, and a plan must be developed by each sales manager for the component of the business for which he or she has responsibility. The territory, account, and opportunity planning is completed by each sales person on the team, and the plans are then consolidated into each sales manager's plan. Assuming you are selling somewhat big-ticket products or services, a general best practice is to have a specific account plan for each of the *accounts* that collectively comprise 70 to 80 percent of the revenue plan and to also have a detailed plan for the top ten or so of the largest *opportunities* for each sales person.

This sounds like a lot of work—and it is. But when executed correctly, a sales plan will cause you to think critically about what must happen during the year in order for the unit to meet its goals. It will force understanding that perhaps you are underresourced, or perhaps you are spending too much time on a prospect or a line of business that does not have sufficient potential and the time would be better spent focused elsewhere. You may learn of new competitive threats. You will get insights on how to better leverage what is working in one scenario for another client or opportunity. Learning where to stop applying resources is just as valuable as deciding on new actions.

Developing a written plan each year is a fundamental sales management necessity. An equally important requirement is keeping the plan up-to-date over the course of the year. Again this is where many organizations fall short. Just as the planning process yields insights and learning during the creation of the plan, similar benefits will come from the time and effort spent going through periodic updates. You may discover that a given strategy is not working, or perhaps you have made no progress thus far on implementing one of the key strategies necessary for a successful year.

Five years ago, a second-stage consumer products company had just kicked off its annual business planning process. This company sells outdoor products mostly through high-end specialty sporting goods and outdoors retailers. As the CEO and the team were talking about the sales plan and tactics for the upcoming year, they came to some important insights regarding changes in their industry. The insights occurred as a by-product of the planning process where the team was engaged in a fairly detailed discussion regarding the specific needs of a number of their largest customers. The increased availability of information was giving more power to suppliers. Better retail systems were making buyers behave differently—placing smaller initial orders, but using their POS systems to expect inventory replenishment from their suppliers on a just-in-time basis. There was consolidation of retailers, giving buyers more buying power. And the near universal adoption of the Internet made it easy for their customers to shop around. The company risked being squeezed by their suppliers and their customers. Its planning process, which began as a sales planning effort, led the company to undertake a fundamental shift in strategy. The company correctly understood that the key to its success was to do one of two things: create a willingness among customers to pay more for its product because of product quality and branding, or reduce cost to compete on price. This story ends well, as the company embarked on a journey to create a series of premium, highly differentiated products that customers have been willing to pay a substantial upcharge for. The company has enjoyed double-digit growth in the category and is viewed as a premium brand.

MEASURE INPUTS

Most companies realize fairly early on the benefits that come from implementing a customer relationship management (CRM) system. Implemented correctly, and after adoption by the sales and marketing people in the company, such a system equips the company to keep track of key customer data; it can provide better and more timely follow-up, keep track of salespersons' activity, and provide the data so that revenue can be forecast more accurately. Analysis of CRM data can also lead to a variety of insights that help the business leaders, including those regarding competitive insights, trends, and effectiveness of marketing programs; in some cases, the analysis will also provide insights into the behavior of key customers. Clearly, CRM systems have been highly useful in raising the bar in the sales area.

This has not been without some drawbacks, however. CRM systems excel at measuring quantitative metrics: what has happened as a result of a given activity. One of the things that I have found helpful is to force managers to spend at least as much time focused on measuring the qualitative inputs in the sales process. Call activity is a good example to consider. The number of calls a salesperson makes each week is an important quantitative input, but the quality of each call is a qualitative metric that defies easy capture by most CRM systems. Many other inputs are more subjective and cannot necessarily be gleaned from any system. Measuring and understanding these inputs requires more work. For example, what percentage of initial calls results in a follow-up call? What was the quality of the conversation during that initial call? What is the quality of the relationship that the salesperson has with the client? How often does the client refer his or her contacts both inside and outside the company to you? What is the quality of the team's written communication? Is the sales team effectively leveraging social media to drive their activity and success? Do the salespeople really understand the subtle and unspoken issues in a company such that they can leverage this knowledge to improve their likelihood of success? Can the salespeople effectively push back and tell clients they are wrong about a given issue? And finally, how often do salespeople help a client by uncovering some issue (and a solution) that the client had not even thought of? Does a trust-based relationship exist with their most important clients? The answers to these and other questions are *inputs* to the sales process that ultimately result in revenue. The successful sales manger knows the answers to these questions for each person on the team. This information does not come out of any system per se. It comes from the manager doing his or her job and paying close attention to all the inputs that make good results possible.

The key learning is that managing the directly inputs is how to affect the outputs. After all, it is very difficult to manage revenue—it is what happens as a result of a successfully executed sales process.

PROVIDE A WRITTEN MONTHLY REVIEW

In my experience, if you want to be sure that your sales managers are doing all they can to measure the inputs to the process, it is extremely helpful to insist that sales managers provide a written review of each salesperson on their team—every month. *Every month? Written? All of the salespeople? Even those that are "stars"?* The answer is a resounding *yes!* The reason is simple. In order to be able to do this review correctly each month, the manager has to be spending time with each of his or her direct reports. That is, you cannot do an effective review from just looking at reports and metrics. This process, while a bit rigid, does require an ongoing dialogue with each of the salespeople on the team beyond the here and now or related to the deal or client of the day. Consistently implementing this practice in each of the start-ups that I have been part of has helped managers have their teams working at peak level.

The keys to the success of this step are deep knowledge of the members of the team and astute time management. Team members who are doing a great job get quality time with their manager, and their behavior and results get positive reinforcement, such as individual coaching and additional support. Often, the good performers are neglected, as spending time with the best people will many times have a large return on the time invested. But if you consider the benefits that come from a discussion of the following points, I think you will agree that there is always much to talk about for those who are struggling as well as for those who are doing well:

- How do you feel about last month?
- What were your top accomplishments?
- What did not happen that you wanted to occur?
- What are your top ten accounts and top ten opportunities now?
- What makes you think these are real and actionable?
- If this is an issue with the client, why has the client not done something about this before?
- If the client acts on this, what is the benefit?
- If the client does nothing, what happens?
- What is the priority of actions in front of the client? Who else do you need to have this happen?
- What are your must-dos for the coming month?
- What help do you need?

Team members who are struggling also get time, but it is spent in a more targeted and constructive way. In the reviews, the manager's reviews point out an ongoing series of activities and effort required on the part of the salesperson to improve. In the subsequent month's session, the execution of those activities becomes a point of discussion during the review.

When you first implement this practice, you will experience significant resistance from your sales managers. They will not want to do this and will try to convince you it is overkill and may demotivate the sales team. But once the practice has taken hold, the effective managers will discover that it actually helps them help their people perform at a much higher level. The individual salespeople will also tell you that the practice is helpful. There is learning that comes from the conversations during the review, but there is also the benefit of receiving suggestions, feedback, and advice *in writing,* every month, that causes a sales professional to take note and attempt to integrate the learning into his or her behavior.

All written reviews should be forwarded to you (or to the second-level manager, if this role exists). When you read these monthly individual packets, they will give you a very good indication of how well the manager is monitoring his or her team. If a consistent poor performance pattern develops, it can be discussed and rectified before it becomes serious.

TALENT MANAGEMENT

Another practice that I have found to be helpful comes straight from my days at GE. Under the leadership of Jack Welch, GE implemented a forced ranking system. Each year, the bottom 10 percent of people in every department across the entire company were let go, so that new people, preferably people who had the potential to be better, could be hired or promoted. Thus, managers were encouraged to be constantly on the lookout for new talent. They had to be because they knew that no matter how well they were doing in any given year, they would still need to recruit new team members. In a relatively short period of time, implementation of this approach led to a step-change increase in revenues and profitability at GE.

In small, rapidly growing entrepreneurial organizations, the consequences of subpar performance are even more dramatic. Waiting until you had a vacant position inevitably led to a poor outcome. However, getting this right, as we discussed in chapter 5, pays enormous benefits.

While most managers agree that poor performers drag down the entire company, they are still way too slow to act and are far too tolerant. Just look at the statistics we discussed earlier. Talk is cheap, but change—true change regarding the vital aspect of sales management—requires action.

Effective managers are realistically critical of their direct reports. They recruit the very best people they can, provide training, support, and coaching, but if someone, for whatever reason, does not achieve at a reasonable level, the manager must act, and quickly, to find a person who will. And the manager must do this with as much kindness, humility, and consideration for the person affected as possible. No good whatsoever comes from anything less than the best behavior as you fire a person from your company.

PARTING WORDS

Effective sales management is one of the best levers to drive second-stage growth. As we have seen elsewhere, identifying a great person for this role is critical. The ideal person has achieved success in a similar selling environment and also has the leadership and management capability that is required to build and manage a cohesive and results-driven team. A true star in this role will insure that he or she has a team that can excel and will work closely with each of the team members every day to drive revenue growth.

Chapter 8

GROWTH MARKETING

THE WORDS *SALES* AND *MARKETING* are often used in the same sentence in business discussions and articles as though they are part of one catchphrase. To many, it may appear as though sales and marketing are just different words for the same or similar activities. After all, the ultimate function of both is to influence a purchase decision. However, this is a misconception and often leads to wasted time and resources. It is important to know the differences between these two business functions to make them work for you. Naturally, as executed within a company, they support the efforts of the company to secure clients and revenue. But that's where the similarities end.

As we've seen, the world of sales is all about selling products or services to qualified customers. Making the contact, understanding the prospect's needs, proposing a solution, and closing the deal are the basic components of the sales process. Without a competent, well-managed, and suitably aggressive sales team, the company can't grow to scale, build revenue, and develop sustained profitability.

But in order for a sales team to be successful, the salespeople also need to have the right products, and the latter must be appropriately priced, packaged, and promoted from a company with a strong industry profile. That's where marketing comes in. Without an integrated, well-planned, and targeted marketing effort, salespeople can find themselves pitching in a vacuum. Marketing creates the context for the products and services. Marketing is integral to the entire company effort. From shaping the initial concept, to the branding, packaging, pricing, and positioning of the product through brochures, websites, and promotional campaigns to thought leadership, speaking engagements, exhibiting at industry conferences, comparative research into competitors—marketing comprises the key elements that put a company on the map. Marketing builds the brand and reinforces the reputation of the company.

As the business world has evolved over the past fifteen years, the importance of effective marketing has skyrocketed for all companies but particularly so for second-stage firms. There are very few second-stage companies that can ignore building an effective marketing plan as a fundamental part of their plan for growth. What companies need from their marketing departments includes basics such as the following:

- analysis of markets and customers to determine potential product/service needs
- creation of a new products and services
- positioning of the product in the market and against competitors/alternatives
- development of product messages and related marketing collateral
- development of a pricing strategy for the product
- development of advertising or public relations strategies to support the product launch
- selection of the best approach and channels to sell the product
- demonstration of how to sell the product for the sales organization
- collection of feedback from customers and prospects to inform future product and marketing efforts

As you can see, just enumerating these items based on the classic 4Ps of marketing—*product, price, place,* and *promotion*—creates quite a long list. But today, in the Internet age, marketing includes other essential activities. Experts in marketing will tell you that in the past 10 years, marketing has been fundamentally transformed.

Paul Rand is the CEO and founder of the Zocolo Group. The Zocolo Group is a word-of-mouth, social, and digital marketing agency. Paul started the company in 2007 with the vision to create a new category in marketing services. Zocolo's view is that your product or firm's brand is not what you say it is; rather, your brand is what your customers and prospects say about your company and its product or service. In other words, if you are trying to push your message into the market, you will lose. Instead, engage in tactics that will result in your clients and other decision influencers talking about and promoting your brand in the marketplace, thus adding credibility to your company. Not only has this new strategy worked for Zocolo's clients, but it has propelled rapid growth for Zocolo as well. The company has grown to over 100 employees since its founding and has built its own brand as an expert in its field.

THE CHANGING WORLD

In the previous chapter, we touched on the notion that the world of selling has been fundamentally altered because customers now are researching your company before, during, and after the sales process. Customers often know quite a bit about your firm or product before they have met with you. Most of this research is done using a variety of online and social media tools and learning what others are saying about your firm as well. Your marketing team is responsible for shaping the information your customers find in their research. Thus, most companies seeking rapid growth have discovered that it is necessary to have marketing capability within the firm that understands search engine optimization (SEO), web site analytics, the mechanics of click-through and bounce rates, and a variety of other marketing technologies and applications that have emerged in the past few years.

Bob Sanders of AXIOM SFD, whom we met in chapter 2, believes that having an effective marketing capability is at least as important a driver of revenue growth for his business as having excellence in sales. And this view is coming from a person who runs a sales training and development business.

Until recently, AXIOM SFD, like many companies just entering the second stage, had an intermittent approach to the implementation of marketing programs. In AXIOM's first stage of growth, Bob, as the CEO, was also effectively the CMO (and the CSO as well). AXIOM tried various sporadic campaigns, approaches, and messages and hoped for some results. As a busy CEO who wore a variety of hats, it was difficult for Bob to oversee a concerted and consistent marketing effort. Bob discovered what many now know: if you are going to have success in developing and executing a successful marketing program, you have to have someone dedicated to the role.

Sales and marketing are both complicated and specialized disciplines. Success in either requires specific expertise, focus, and dedicated application and management of the strategy and the plan. He discovered that marketing is a mission critical function, and successful execution could not be ensured on a part time basis. He further realized that even though he had extensive marketing experience earlier in his career, both the art and science of marketing had changed so much that he really needed a person who is completely up-to-date with all of the new technology that has been developed specifically targeted at the marketing function.

Today, as a result of significantly increasing the allocation of resources to AXIOM's marketing efforts, more than half of the firm's revenue begins with leads that have resulted from specific marketing activities. The company discovered a truth that many other enterprises have learned: a more systematic approach to lead generation becomes critical to growth. AXIOM's marketing efforts begin with content generation. The goal of content generation is to insure the firm ends up on a potential buyer's consideration set. The company's marketing team makes sure that potential customers see valuable and timely content that has been created by AXIOM and serves to educate and inform clients. This effort clears the path for the sales team to emphasize the value of their products in solving their clients' needs.

INVEST IN MARKETING EARLY

As you think about how marketing can help your growth plan, you first have to decide on the right time to hire a person to do this. This is not an easy decision in that committing to a full-time marketing manager and the subsequent marketing plan will require a substantial investment. However, when fashioning your business plan from the start, it is important to consider marketing a necessary investment to drive growth. Most make the mistake of investing in marketing well after they should have done so, and thus they miss out on an opportunity to augment the growth plan from the start.

Marketing plans depend on the nature of your business and your industry. In the world of B2B services, the goal of marketing is more focused on establishing the reputation and brand of the company. Marketing's role then is about providing advice and guidance regarding the company's central message. Products and pricing concerns follow in the wake of establishing your company as the primary source for solutions in whatever arena you service.

Heidi O'Gorman is the managing partner of Carrick Marketing. Her firm is focused on helping small and midsize professional services firms grow through effective, customized marketing strategies. Heidi cut her teeth in the business services world at Arthur Andersen, LLP, and Deloitte Consulting. Heidi has a strong view on the role marketing should play as a firm enters the second stage. She believes that it is important to have professional marketing expertise early in the evolution of the company.

Without dedicated marketing capability, the sales organization will fill the vacuum and decide on the brand and the approach to the market on their own. Focused on selling and closing deals, the sales team may chase a number of prospects that are not a good fit as potential customers, thus wasting time and effort. Further issues arise when each salesperson in each geographical region portrays the company and its products or services in a different way; as a result, the brand and reputation of the company are not clearly defined for the market.

In the early days of a company's existence the goal is to promote a point of view on the appropriate brand message. As the company establishes itself in the marketplace and gains momentum, the smart marketing expert will work to keep it responsive to changes in the industry and keep it authoritative. Sometimes, a message that sounds good to the founder and management team does not work at all with potential customers. The brand message must be clear and compelling and provide a point of differentiation from alternatives. It has to resonate with the targeted recipients of the message. Often this requires reevaluation and adjustment to meet current trends.

But marketing also provides an independent effort within a company. Quantifying the financial impact marketing programs have on the bottom line is vital to creating a successful program. Using a CRM system along with some human judgment, it is possible to track leads and the revenue that results from marketing activities. What was the source of each lead? Did it come from an industry conference, a speaking engagement, an article, from a thought leadership email campaign, from SEO, or from an advertisement?

Where Heidi has implemented this quantified approach for her clients, she finds overwhelmingly that effective marketing campaigns generate a high return on investment. Revenue directly attributed to marketing activities often exceeds the cost of the entire marketing budget, including the personnel costs of the group.

A few years ago after selling his advertising agency TFA to the Leo Burnett Company, Sean Bisceglia decided to acquire a majority interest in CPRi, a struggling staffing business providing creative and marketing personnel, from its private equity owner. Sean overhauled the sales organization, and this action clearly played a large role in the company's dramatic growth. But Sean, with his roots in marketing and advertising, also was able to leverage an effective marketing strategy as a major component of the growth strategy.

Prior to Sean's arrival, the firm really had no marketing strategy. One of CPRi's early challenges was to convince marketing executives in client companies that the use of "freelance" talent in the marketing area was a smart practice. At the time, this just was not done. Typically, CMO's would turn either to in-house expertise or to an agency. Agencies can provide tremendous value, but they can also be very expensive, especially for the requisite basic marketing tactics. Hiring the right marketing expert instead of an agency is a cost-effective alternative and could be customized to a company's unique needs.

CPRi worked hard to promote the new category of "marketing staffing." The company's marketing efforts showcased large companies using freelance labor from CPRi to help achieve their marketing objectives. CPRi became active in industry associations and trade shows, and Sean was a frequent speaker. All of CPRi's collateral information was redone, which resulted in positioning the firm as a highly creative thought leader in the market. The SEO segment of its marketing plan also had a significant impact by driving talented freelance consultants to CPRi that the company could hire and deploy to clients and by appealing to firms that were looking for marketing support. In the course of the next two years, CPRi grew from just $4 million to nearly $30 million and was subsequently sold to Aquent, a large marketing and creative staffing firm based in Boston.

THREE GOALS OF GROWTH MARKETING

In the second stage of growth, it pays if marketing just sticks to the basics. These basics include three primary areas of marketing activity. The first is the brand. The key goal here is making your brand stand out in the market place. Michael Lies, one of the nation's leading brand strategists, believes that in marketing your brand, you need to make the customer the "hero" of his or her story. In other words, the story should tell how customers found and used the product or service to overcome a problem or issue and became a "hero" by doing so.

The trick is to figure out how to create content around your product or brand that can serve as a story or provide the feeling of an experience. Michael Lies uses the example of the dramatic growth of Red Bull, fed in part by the brand promoting people doing crazy stunts and then broadcasting those stunts to their friends. In addition, Red Bull sponsored extreme sporting events featuring cliff diving, BMX racing, wakeboarding, motorcycle racing, connecting their brand to these adventurous athletes. They produced and distributed high-quality, full-length films of extreme, high-risk activities such as heli-snowboarding. Red Bull became an integral part of the story as it helped fuel these stunts with its high-energy contents.

Shiftgig has also been quite effective in leveraging this same tactic. Shiftgig is a pure technology company offering a social media software platform to match the right employer with the right applicant. The company's marketing efforts make extensive use of stories highlighting individuals who found a "perfect job" through the Shiftgig platform and employers who found Shiftgig a superior recruiting tool for talent. These stories are on the Shiftgig website, are used in email marketing, and appear prominently in social media such as Twitter and Facebook.

The second basic goal of growth marketing is increasing your company's footprint, i.e., its reputation and recognition value in the market. One way to accomplish this goal is to make your company a thought leader in your market or industry. Designate spokespeople who deliver presentations at industry events, write articles and books on significant developments in the industry, or take on inspirational speaking engagements. In effect, your firm will appear at the forefront of the industry, the go-to source for information and expertise.

You will appear to the market and to potential customers to be substantially larger than you really are. Thought leadership delivered effectively as part of your marketing and public relations efforts reaps big results by opening doors to new opportunities and clients.

Another way to increase your footprint is to target high-profile prospects and acquire them as customers. As satisfied clients with good stories to tell about your company, they can be integrated into your marketing message. If you can provide solutions to very large clients, small to midsized clients will take notice. This strategy worked for HarQen, the recruitment screening technology firm we learned about in chapter 4.

As HarQen was building its reputation for cutting-edge web telephony technology for screening and recruiting, the company originally was going to market its service to primarily to Fortune 500 companies, as these companies recruit significant numbers of new employees each year. But then management realized that the "whales" of recruiting were not Fortune 500 firms but rather the top staffing and consulting firms. Each of the top global staffing firms hires millions of people each year. Manpower, for example, hires nearly 4 million people per year.[1] For each person hired, about three to five potential candidates must be screened.

The founder of HarQen, Kelly Fitzsimmons, specifically targeted the top three providers of staffing services in part to obtain the revenue that could come from these huge firms. But they did so also because by securing these firms as clients, HarQen would demonstrate that its new technology can be an effective tool in handling all volumes of recruitment efforts efficiently and personally. As the large staffing firms became customers, the implicit market value of this third-party endorsement enhanced HarQen's industry footprint, and it still continues to fuel second-stage growth.

The third goal of growth marketing is conveying a clear and consistent message. As the firm grows and new individuals and clients are added into the mix, the overall profile of your company and products can become diffuse. Newly hired people often come with their own perspective on what is important, on how services should be positioned and delivered, and on what aspect of the success needs to be highlighted. The marketing group needs to get involved early in growth efforts to make sure that new product or services and new people are integrated into the brand message in a consistent fashion. In some ways, marketing has to be the guardian of clarity and consistency.

MARKETING YOUR MESSAGE

If your company sells a product as opposed to a service, marketing is even more important to driving revenue than in a classic service business. In product marketing, you must first determine to whom the product is sold. Is there more than one category of buyer? Is the buyer of the product the user of the product? After you determine who the buyers are, the next goal is to determine how best to reach them. Some key questions to ask are:

- What channel will be most effective for delivering the message?
- What content, both logical and emotional, will influence buyers' purchase decisions?
- What is the most effective message or set of messages that will influence the buying decision?
- Are there others influencing the purchase decision whom you must reach as well?

Mindy Meade is a former advertising industry executive and currently the managing partner of Strategic Marketing Associates. Prior to starting her own firm, she had an extensive career with the Leo Burnett agency, working with companies trying to build brands. She uses a simple outline to show the essentials around which an effective marketing organization should organize its efforts:

CONVINCE: *The target client or customer*
THAT: *What you want them to believe*
BECAUSE: *What the benefits are, both rational and emotional*

As this spare but insightful template shows, effective marketing stays focused on the concrete concerns of the client acquisition process. Who are you targeting (and must be specific in this definition)? How do you reach these people? What features and benefits are they likely to value? What is the message that will appeal to your targeted audience, both from a rational and an emotional point of view?

Once you have determined the target audience and have a message you believe will appeal to this audience, then you can decide the best channel to reach the audience that is affordable within your growth plan.

As mentioned earlier, one frequent mistake is the tendency for executives to pick a method to deliver a message that is based more on their own subjective view of what will work, rather than on a carefully considered and fact-based selection process. An example would be placing a full page ad in a prestigious magazine or newspaper that appeals to the image the executive wants for the company rather than using an approach that might be less glamorous but far more effective. Another example would be paying large sponsorship fees to have your product included in a TV program or perhaps a sporting event when this does little to impact the specific message you must deliver to your intended audience.

Usually the time-honored tactics work best. Of course, what these are depends on the product but would include effective use of public relations, speaking, thought leadership, and attendance and participation at relevant industry conferences and trade shows. For example, consider what put the Founders Brewing Co. on the map—the founders attended the beer conference Extreme Beer Festival. Their success there led to press coverage of the specific products they were making, which led to buzz in the online beer lovers world, and this ultimately made the Founders Brewing brand one that was increasingly sought out by beer lovers. It was not a multimillion dollar advertising campaign that drove their success. It was a grassroots effort, perfectly suited to the company's target market, brilliantly executed, with a bit of luck and good fortune added into the mix.

MBO Partners can serve as another example of how to orchestrate an effective marketing campaign unique to a company and clients. The firm offers several different kinds of services to three different categories of clients: owners of small businesses, midsized companies, and large corporations. Each service and client has a different set of goals and needs, and MBO developed marketing strategies to reach each one. While founder Gene Zaino believes that brand and reputation matter, he has found that they matter less on the B2B enterprise side of his business that services huge companies. He feels they can support the brand through both specific and targeted direct sales and marketing tactics rather than through more general brand-building efforts.

For its enterprise business, marketing's focus is to make sure MBO Partners is present and visible at the places where these customers are. The company executives know who their customers are likely to be, and they know where these customers are located in the marketplace. Using this information, they can engage in outreach strategies to contact these potential customers and also make it easy for potential clients to reach out to MBO Partners. MBO is a member of various industry associations and is active at trade shows; the company also sponsors key industry events and workshops. The firm wants to be in front of the enterprise buyer, pure and simple. Thus, marketing for this side of the business is focused on more traditional tactics.

MBO Partners also has a small business consumer side to its business. This business looks more like a B2C product purchase than an enterprise service selling effort. The number of potential customers for this part of their business is well into the millions, so the only way to tackle a market of this size is to draw potential customers to MBO. Here, MBO's brand is critical. The challenge for the management team was to figure out how to scale the notion of "trust." After the company had worked out the strategy to reach a large segment of this customer base, the momentum of the success stories extended the brand to other consumers.

PARTING WORDS

Sales and marketing are complementary, not interchangeable activities. Marketing gives sales the tools they need to effectively sell. It provides a story to tell, a strategy for reaching the widest possible range of prospects and to keep the company's brand and profile front and center in the marketplace. Second-stage marketers focus on the basics. They will understand who your customers are. They will understand the message that must be delivered to build credibility and gain the trust of these customers. They will know the message that works best and the most effective channel for delivering it. And as the company grows, markets change and products evolve, marketers will stay on task to change, refine, and improve the marketing strategy and its execution as necessary.

Growth marketing is a significant factor in success. Often this decision can be counterintuitive for the second-stage entrepreneur. Resources are usually tight. In most cases, entrepreneurs have achieved success already by relying on aggressive sales of their unique product or service. Marketing seems like an abstract activity that may not be worth the investment. However, if you talk with second-stage entrepreneurs who have successfully made the journey to sustained growth, almost to a person they will tell you they should have spent more time and more money on marketing early on. The dedicated marketing strategy, supervised by the right professional, will be a significant lever in the effort to drive your company to hypergrowth. Make it part of your business growth plan from day one and reap the rewards.

Chapter 9

THE TOTAL CUSTOMER EXPERIENCE

MOST PEOPLE UNDERSTAND THAT GREAT companies—the ones we talk about, write about, and are passionate about—base much of their ongoing success on what is called *the total customer experience*. From the first contact to final fulfillment, these companies make sure that every interaction with their customers delivers satisfaction. They have made this part of their cultural DNA; they understand that a commitment to an exemplary level of customer service is vital to success because the best spokesperson for any business is a completely satisfied customer.

There are a limited number of companies that have been able to successfully implement a total customer service approach as a key strategy fueling their growth. The few companies of scale that consistently deliver on this premise are well known and include iconic names such as Amazon, Apple, Ritz Carlton, Zappos, Lexus, Federal Express, and Nordstrom. As customers of these businesses, we know that their approach is the exception in the world today, not the norm. Of course, these companies are now quite large, but they were once second-stage companies and in some cases not that long ago. Amazon, for example, was a start-up in 1994, Zappos in 1999. These companies' long-term commitment to provide a superlative total customer experience differentiates them from their competitors and has put them on top.

These companies have created an entire organization devoted to creating one-on-one relationships with their customers, no small task since they are involved in thousands or even millions of transactions per day. From complete transparency of the product information to helpful employees, from competitive product pricing to efficient service, each of these companies has allocated resources to engineering a system that gives the customer the best experience possible. To a great extent, these companies' attention to the details of each customer's needs has become one of the identifying qualities of their brands.

THE GREAT DIVIDE IN TOTAL CUSTOMER EXPERIENCE

As important as the total customer experience is to the success of any company, it is surprising how few companies invest the management time and capital to make it part of their operating principles. Keep in mind that we are talking about the total customer experience, not simply a specific aspect of it such as customer service or merchandizing. The total customer experience is more complex, which is probably the reason why so many companies fail to deliver it successfully.

In their book *The Customer Experience Revolution* (Raphel Marketing, 2011), Jeofrey Bean and Sean Van Tyne estimate that only 5 percent of all US organizations value, let alone deliver, exceptional customer experience. According to a CEI Survey, 86 percent of buyers will pay more for a better customer experience. But only 1 percent of customers feel that vendors consistently meet their expectations.[1] And this is for *meeting* expectations, not exceeding them, which is the goal you should strive to accomplish if you want to generate customer loyalty. These are indeed appalling statistics in light of the enormous research done over the past 20 years that conclusively proves that there is a compelling and direct link between the ability to consistently deliver a high-quality customer experience and growth and profits. In their book, Green and Van Tyne cite Forrester research as showing that the top 10 customer service leaders generated returns that were 41 percent better than the S&P 500 Index. They further point out that over a three-year period, the customer experience leaders' returns were 145 percent better than those of the group of companies that were the customer service laggards. So contrary to what some companies think, providing an exceptional customer experience each and every time can lead to a consistently high return on the investment.

Customers' time and money are precious. If they can count on a beneficial experience with a company, they will pay a premium for it. They will remain loyal, return for repeat business, and most important, recommend the company to others. It's a win-win from beginning to end for a company smart enough to make providing exceptional customer experience a priority.

TOTAL CUSTOMER EXPERIENCE ACCELERATES GROWTH

But what does this all have to do with being a second-stage entrepreneur looking to drive a business to rapid growth? In a word: opportunity. In chapter 3, I discussed the concept of "create, don't compete" as a powerful way to differentiate your company from others in the marketplace. Delivering a unique total customer experience is one way to leapfrog over the competition. Given the overwhelmingly weak attention paid to this important concept as demonstrated by the research cited above, you can implement the strategy of providing a total customer experience as a stepping-stone to second-stage success.

Unlike larger, more rigid competitors, smart start-ups can afford to be more responsive to their customers and make their experience with the company so memorable that they will be coming back for more and tell their friends and colleagues. Indeed, many entrepreneurs have leveraged this gap by creating smaller enterprises that deliver a compelling product or service in a special, totally client-centric way unavailable from their competitors.

For example, consider the growth of boutique hotels, niche executive search firms, or a high-end bicycle company such as Seven. These companies have correctly figured out that their clients want an individualized service and are willing to pay for it, provided it is delivered with attention to their needs. This is the total customer experience customers can't get from larger competitors focused on volume and overall market share.

For a more detailed example, let's go back to Intelligentsia Coffee and Tea to see what is involved in the total customer experience. At Intelligentsia, everything is about the quality of the total coffee experience: where it is sourced, how it is blended and roasted, how long it stays in packages, the welcoming and unique ambience of the retail locations, and most important, how the coffee is served to each retail customer, one cup at a time to order with a smile. The baristas do not pour your cup from a big pot. Rather, you have a choice of customer blends, which are measured, ground fresh, and brewed while you wait. You get all this for a premium price well beyond that of Starbucks or Dunkin Donuts. At Intelligentsia Coffee and Tea customers pay for the quality of coffee, to be sure, but what they are really devoted to is the total customer experience they get every time they enter an Intelligentsia retail location. Consistently of high quality, efficient, and friendly, this experience has become Intelligentsia's principal commodity and brand identifier.

MAKING THE COMMITMENT

Providing the total customer experience is like every other important element in your plan to grow your successful start-up. Attention to each of the details involved in the process will make or break your success. When you're building your company and expanding your client base, any miscalculation can have disastrous effects, especially one regarding the customer experience. Some key questions to answer as you focus your attention on these issues include:

- What kind of experience does the customer want?
- Does the company deliver this experience now?

- What culture changes are necessary to ensure the company delivers an exceptional experience?
- What resources need to be allocated to this effort in terms of personnel, delivery, payment systems, and follow-up?
- How can success be measured?
- How can success be promoted to become part of the brand?

For just as customers will rave about the things you get right, they will just as quickly take notice of things you forgot. And in today's world, they will tell others—in conversations, over coffee, and on social media.

It's hard to get all the details right every time because everyone in the entire system has to understand the need to consistently perform at a high level—and the entire system really includes everyone in your company. This works only if there are no gaps. Total customer experience means total company commitment. After asking the basic questions, you will need to create a plan to deliver the best customer experience possible. Below is a general guideline to help you think about how to create and execute such a plan.

MAKE TOTAL CUSTOMER EXPERIENCE A TOP PRIORITY

Making total customer experience a priority is an important first step and must come from the founder and be supported by the senior management team. There has to a commitment of funds and resources to follow through and a commitment that the management processes, incentives, and disincentives all support the mission.

RESEARCH THE PREVAILING BEST PRACTICES IN THE MARKETPLACE

In order to create a total customer experience that is new and different, you need to know what your competitors are providing to their customers. Research their systems. Look at the customer comments their websites. Understand existing technology that supports the process. Assimilate what works and use it as you revamp your own plan.

CREATE A ROADMAP OF EACH STEP OF THE CUSTOMER EXPERIENCE

The process begins with a detailed description of the current customer experience. You'll need to evaluate the effectiveness of each step and decide which should stay, which need to be changed or enhanced, and which should be dropped. Using this analysis as a starting point, build the entire process to make it stronger, faster, and more satisfying. Get input from the staff interacting with clients: sales, customer service, fulfillment, etc. Canvass your loyal customers for suggestions.

DEFINE THE EXPERIENCE UNIQUE TO YOUR COMPANY

This is a fun phase that also involves most of your senior team and likely also people in the various functions. It is a bit of a brainstorming session. What can your company offer customers that isn't being offered already? The process might begin with asking questions: what is unique about your company and its products? How can you create a customer experience that reflects the character of the company? This could involve some kind of special packaging or a combination of personalized services or a creative discount schedule or payment plan.

REMOVE OBSTACLES TO THE EXPERIENCE

Focus on the aspects of your internal systems that make customer transactions cumbersome or frustrating. Perhaps outsourcing call center functions did not work out as planned or volume has created long wait times to connect. Perhaps faulty packaging or complicated credit qualifying systems frustrate customers. Any parts of the experience customers have complained about have to be revamped to improve the customer experience.

Recently, I interacted with a brand-new technology company marketing a new survey technology product. The product was very compelling, priced right, and perfect for supporting a particular client of mine. However, the company required the customer to read through and agree to a 27-page service agreement with more than a few objectionable provisions. Needless to say, this part of the process did not give me faith in my relationship with the vendor and did not contribute to positive total customer experience. I decided to use a different vendor with a much more streamlined and friendly service agreement.

STRENGTHEN CUSTOMER SUPPORT

Probably one of the most important parts of the total customer experience is how your company supports customers after they have received the product or service. While most customer support systems are designed to deal with questions or problems arising after the transaction has been made, some attention needs to be paid to the front end of the process as well. Paying attention to the customer's needs at both ends of the interaction is critical to the success of the total customer experience. Leaders in the field pay particular attention to training their personnel in customer support and give them considerable latitude in finding solutions to customer issues.

ENSURE REPEAT BUSINESS WITH FOLLOW-UP AND FEEDBACK

As you embark on the journey to providing total customer experience, you will have many opportunities to stay in touch with your customer and gather valuable feedback. The most successful way to underscore the total customer experience is to follow up with customers to let them know you appreciated their business and stand ready to help with any future needs. This cements your relationship with them and rounds out their experience with your company.

Assembling feedback is also important for keeping your company performing at peak. This feedback will come from customers, employees, suppliers, and potentially also from others, such as investors, media, and competitors. This information comes in variety of forms: written, spoken, and digital. It can take the form of complaints or praise, gratitude for a job well done or criticism pointing out what needs to change. Each and every bit of feedback is vital to the process. Often it is useful to go a step further by soliciting feedback through customer surveys. There is also an emerging field of social media monitoring. There are a variety of tools designed to help you keep up-to-date and monitor what your customers are saying about your firm online.

RE-INNOVATE

Total customer experience is a moving target. The marketplace is constantly changing due to technology and the introduction of new strategies. To be fully committed to delivering a great customer experience, you need to be vigilant. Use the feedback you get, raise the bar to improve upon the experience, and pay attention to what is happening in the marketplace. Put a regular review process in place to correct any glitches in the system.

Shiftgig has a very different total customer experience to deal with than what traditional companies face. Nearly all interactions Shiftgig is likely to have with a customer are virtual. The company operates entirely in an online world. Technology companies have learned to deal with this challenge. In the case of Shiftgig, even though it is really just entering its second stage of growth, the company has well-developed practices and dedicated people to insure delivery of a total customer experience that is superlative. They have hired a "community manager." The job of this person is to reach out to users, both individuals who are looking for work and hiring managers, to get specific feedback on what is working well and where improvements

can be made. Sometimes the community manager provides unsolicited feedback to random specific users on how they can make their
profile better, and she also sends out automated surveys on a regular
basis to get various users' perspective. As in most technology companies, Shiftgig's product development is never done. Shiftgig rolls out
new features continuously, as often as twice a week. Sometimes, after
getting customer feedback, the company finds it needs to revert to a
previous version if some new feature receives negative feedback or
does not seem to work as well as planned.

Shiftgig has also hired a different person who is responsible to
keep track of all the online conversations about Shiftgig. This person also works to establish and sustain Shiftgig's presence on Twitter
and Facebook. It is interesting to note that this person started in the
role when Shiftgig was a two-month-old company. This shows the
importance the company's founders placed on ensuring that the total
customer experience is as good as it can be.

As I think about the companies I have been a part of, certainly one
of the aspects that helped drive rapid growth was some understanding
of the power of the total customer experience and making this experience better than some of the client's alternatives and choices. I participated in an executive seminar at the Harvard Business School while
I was in my first start-up, and the learning from that course, entitled
"The Service-Profit Chain," profoundly affected my thinking about
the power that comes from focusing on delivering a high-quality customer experience. The Harvard professors who taught that executive
seminar had spent five years researching the practices of a number
of companies to attempt to correlate the linkage between profit and
growth on the one hand and customer loyalty, customer satisfaction,
employee satisfaction, and productivity on the other. According to
the book, *The Service-Profit Chain* by Earl Sasser, James Heskett, and
Leonard Schlesinger (HBS Press, 1997), the chain is connected as follows: Profit and growth are a result of high levels of customer loyalty.

Loyalty is a direct result of customer satisfaction. Satisfaction results when customers perceive a high level of value in the goods and services provided. Value is most influenced by loyal, productive, and happy employees. Employee satisfaction results primarily from enlightened and logical support services and policies that enable employees to deliver results to customers without having to obtain management permission each and every time. The service-profit chain is also defined by a special kind of leadership that emphasizes the importance of each employee and customer.[2] What was brilliant about the research was that the authors were able to quantitatively prove that firms consistently performing in this fashion, with these practices, significantly outpaced their peer group in growth and profit. The big mystery, of course, all these years later, is why there are not more companies that have embraced the strategy and practices laid out in this book.

As we built the start-up companies that followed, we tried to put into practice what we had learned from the Harvard professors as well as what seems intuitively obvious. For example, as mentioned earlier, in these start-up companies, a great deal of attention was paid to who we hired, in the belief that if you don't get this right, you are doomed from the start, and it will be impossible to consistently deliver a great customer experience. If you do nothing else, get this right. Great employees will often overcome significant obstacles placed in front of them by their own companies to keep customers happy, and they do this entirely on their own. And in keeping with the definition of the total customer experience, where every potential touchpoint between a customer and your company matters, it follows that every person in the company matters. There are no second-class citizens. Engagement levels of employees are critically important. How a random phone call to the company is answered matters. How the staff is dressed matters. How a sales call is conducted matters. How an issue with a client is handled matters. How a consultant delivers a difficult message matters, and this is a skill all consultants must master.

How well the management team understands that its job is to help the team be successful is critical. Most fundamentally, it is important to understand how a client perceives value, which is defined as the cost or investment required for the product or service compared to the outcome that is delivered. It is equally important how satisfied a client is, which is defined as the expectation compared to what is actually delivered. We tried to deliver on all of the above, every day. This is no small task, and we did not meet our goal every day and with every client. But the focus on trying to do this and getting it largely right, paid off handsomely in helping to drive the rapid growth of these companies.

VALUE PERCEPTION MATTERS

Fundamental to delivering the best total customer experience is understanding what your customer perceives as *valuable*. Product quality, competitive pricing, solid customer service, customer support, follow-up are all key components of the experience, but which is of paramount importance to your customers? Using the feedback mechanisms you put in place, analyze the data to determine what your customers really want in their experience with your company and adjust your procedures accordingly.

Customers' expectations of the total customer experience are the other side of their perception of value. Customers bring their experiences with other companies to the relationship with your company. These experiences create an expectation for a certain level of excellence inherent in the customer experience. Anticipating this expectation based on data accumulation through feedback and market research will help you manage the customer experience effectively.

When you can deliver on the total customer experience, you have considerable pricing power, as your customers are buying based on value. For example, if you are a loyal SoulCycle customer and take two classes each week, you could for the same money buy two new carbon fiber bicycles each year. To many people, that would be very sweet. But the SoulCycle founders correctly figured out that their customers' desire for "exercise" is just part of what was valued when taking a spinning class. They correctly choreographed the perfect mix of aerobic exercise, instructor appearance and personality, ambience, music, and heat as well as the other participants that are part of the deal that comes with a SoulCycle class. It is the total customer experience that keeps SoulCycle customers coming back—and coming back frequently.

Likewise, when Founders Brewing concocts a new variety of beer, the company is not really worried about the cost of producing this beer. The owners know that if they have correctly figured out the taste of the beer and can come up with their appropriately creative branding and packaging of the beer, they will have the latitude to add their normal and desired markup to the cost of producing the beer. To be able to successfully pull this off is not at all common; it takes creativity, consistent execution of the strategy, and the ability to connect with customers to deliver an experience that delights them throughout the transaction cycle.

PARTING WORDS

The total customer experience is of paramount importance to the successful growth of your company. It goes far beyond the simple notion of friendly order taking, efficient product or service delivery, or customer support. The total customer experience is the entire process of your company interacting with its customers, from first contact to follow-up and gathering feedback. Delivering a superlative experience will result in loyal clients, repeat business, and expansion through word-of-mouth (or social networks) advertising to a growing number of customers.

Huge companies like Amazon, Apple, or Nordstrom have raised the bar for all companies concerning the level of the total customer experience. They have made the customer experience an important part of their brand identity. As a result, second-stage entrepreneurs wanting to push their successful start-ups to the next level of success have to make a deep commitment to making their customer experience as strong as possible. To achieve this important milestone, everyone needs to pitch in, from the CEO to all employees. The board and investors must also be supportive of the strategy. The current customer experience needs to be defined and analyzed. Goals must be set to streamline the delivery process, reinforce each step to make it as user-friendly and customer-centric as possible.

But once the revamped system is in place, the work doesn't end. Equally important is putting a mechanism in place to measure success and gather constructive feedback. Strengthening and refining the total customer experience is an ongoing activity.

However, the results are worth the investment in training and systems management. Research shows that companies that make the total customer experience a top priority see double-digit increases in revenue and profitability. For a second-stage company building its brand as a serious alternative in a crowded marketplace, providing its clients a unique and satisfying customer experience is the cornerstone to sustained profit and growth.

Chapter 10

CULTURE MATTERS

AT FIRST, THE CONCEPT OF CORPORATE culture might seem a bit too abstract for any discussion of the fast-paced, brass-tacks process of bringing a company to second-stage growth. After all, is this concept of a company's "character" or, as *Entrepreneur* magazine defines it, "a blend of the values, beliefs, taboos, symbols, rituals, and myths" too subjective to make a difference?[1]

For a business to grow to the second stage generally requires that the culture of the business is consistent with the vision and values of the founder and the senior team. It was this vision that created the success of the start-up in the first place. I believe that the culture of a company is the glue that cements the people to the operating strategy, the "secret sauce" that keeps the team focused on the big picture of accelerated growth, and as such it is critically important to consider as part of the overall second-stage growth strategy.

The culture of a business will profoundly impact the company's performance over time. Thus, it is a worthwhile exercise to spend time to codify the values, beliefs, symbols, and behaviors that make up the existing culture and then put in place measures that create and reinforce a "conscious culture" throughout the company. Once this is clearly stated and accepted by all employees, the journey to sustained growth is assured. However, what constitutes a healthy corporate culture? While consistency with the founder's vision and values is certainly the bedrock of health, there are significant qualities that contribute to the overall health of a company's culture. Some of the key aspects are as follows:

- a long-term view of the world
- an understanding that success of the individual depends on the success of the team

- a commitment to deliver a customer experience that equals or exceeds the brand's promise
- an emphasis on doing the right thing, not the expedient thing
- the values of honesty, transparency, and best practices regarding employees and clients
- a policy to hire people who espouse the company culture to build its future

Consider the culture in place at MBO Partners, a firm we referred to earlier in the book. Gene Zaino, the founder and CEO, has worked hard to establish and then evolve a conscious culture that he believes will support growth in the business over the long haul. One of the important elements of this culture is openness and transparency. Gene encourages anyone in the company to walk into his office and make a suggestion or offer constructive criticism. If the person proves correct in his or her assessment, things can and do change. While this openness is not without some issues, of course, employees at MBO feel that they all have a real voice in the company. Turnover is very low, the team remains engaged and committed, and the company has enjoyed sustained growth.

In most businesses, the culture is established by the founders early on and evolves naturally as the business grows and other team members are added. It is an organic process, relying on a willingness to respond to factors that might move the original culture toward dynamic and positive changes.

For example, in a technology business, the culture that evolves is typically centered on the product and innovation. Out of necessity, technical brilliance and innovation are valued above other disciplines. It would be unusual for a technology company to have a culture focused on sales early on. In the beginning, at least, there is typically more passion for the actual product than there is for selling the product. Further, the work environment is casual; the communication style is informal, and there is an emphasis on creating a sense of community and collaboration among team members.

Similarly, in a consulting business, the cultural underpinnings of the business tend to be based on the nature of the deliverables to clients, i.e., the consultants themselves. Often based on the unique personality of the founder, the culture evolves to support a variety of personalities ready to address the needs of clients. The culture of a consulting firm will tend to value interesting projects and an opportunity to learn.

Founder's Brewing Co. is an example of a culture that emphasizes the close community the founders have created. The employees at Founders are referred to as the Founders Family. Every person in the company has his or her photo on the web site. A great deal of time and effort has gone into building a team that is passionate about beer and about being part of a rapidly growing company that makes world-class products for the enjoyment of their customers.

Similarly, the culture at Brandtrust reflects the type of work the company performs for its clients. Because the firm is in the business of creating insights for clients, it takes a certain type of person to fit in well at Brandtrust. They try to hire individuals who are thinkers, who are curious about everything. Daryl Travis, the founder, calls them seekers. They always want to know why, how come, what if. Many of the team members have a background as social scientists, or they were journalists, architects, or authors. Travis is very sensitive to the issue of culture, and it is important to him to focus his time and effort on getting this right. After all, the company focuses on brands. Brands are, in fact, a promise to a stakeholder. Travis believes that brands have higher order ideals; they aspire to be part of something that matters; that is the reason they exist. In a similar fashion, he believes a business can have a higher purpose than just serving clients; he believes that people want to and can make a difference in the world. He believes that he can build the culture at Brandtrust in such a way that his employees can help their clients create better products and improve people's lives.

As you enter the second stage of growth, you need to think about how the existing culture will need to evolve to reflect the changes that will take place. What aspects of the culture do you think are healthy? Are there aspects to your culture that you think are holding you back? Is there a reluctance to charge into the unknown or to push the envelope? Is the culture supportive of challenging the status quo?

How can you create a conscious culture that will evolve with the company at it grows? The key is to define the culture you wish to establish and then go about the process of doing so in a systematic fashion.

After two successful start-ups, I had come to the conclusion that the corporate culture in place in those firms played an important part in our success. As a result, when I co-founded Capital H Group, my third start-up, I began to think more proactively about the kind of culture that was important to me as CEO and also to the entire senior team. I felt it was so important that I made the creation of a conscious company culture part of the original business plan.

In fact, this plan to create a conscious culture from the launch was an important factor in recruiting new team members. They had been dissatisfied with the cultures that permeated their prior huge, global consultancies and wanted to participate in building a culture of their own, one that was healthy and positive. Capital H represented an alternative, a place where their view could help shape the culture. Figure 10.1 gives you an overview of how to create a conscious culture either from start-up or when planning to go to the second stage.

The idea of forming a conscious culture is to start with a given set of inputs, which include the mission and strategy of the business. For example, if you have a product-focused company that is driven by technological innovation, you will likely need a very different culture

Figure 10.1   Conscious culture development model

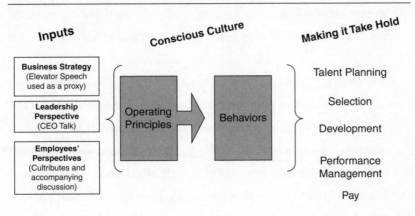

than if you run a retail business that is based on a point-of-purchase model. The first step is to understand the fundamental nature of your company. Once you can articulate what kind of company you have created and have defined the existing culture, you will have an easier time in crafting any changes for a conscious culture designed for growth.

The most significant perspectives regarding your culture are those of the leaders and employees. Each of these groups will have different ideas about the corporate culture. In some cases, it might be useful to bring trusted customers into the process and get their views as well. They may even be able to articulate what changes in the conscious culture they would value as customers. In order to create a successful conscious culture, these perspectives need to be integrated.

Once you have gathered clear and concrete data from each group (the far left column in figure 10.1), then I suggest you go through a process of discussing and prioritizing a set of operating principles and desired behaviors (the center column in figure 10.1) with representatives from the existing team.

A conscious culture is primarily a value-based one as opposed to a rule-based one. The goal is to ensure that everyone is clear about the fundamental values and strategic goals. Of course, there needs to be some basic framework of systems and directives to reinforce the values. Depending upon the nature of your business, a successful conscious culture will end up being a combination of both values and rules.

After you agree on set of operating principles, you can then discuss a list of behaviors that you would value as a team to support the operating principles. For example, in the case of Capital H Group, we particularly wanted a highly collaborative work ethic to pervade the organization. We wanted to reward contribution and effort with recognition as opposed to status or hierarchy. As result, the team became self-supporting and self-governing with checks and balances geared to performance that helped the entire team.

The efforts to create a conscious culture for future growth will gain little traction if there are no guidelines in place for rewarding and reinforcing the culture for team members. It is critical to think about and implement mechanisms that put teeth into policies and behavioral standards expected in the conscious culture. One of the more difficult aspects in supporting a conscious culture is what to do when a person is performing at a high level, generating fantastic results, but does not respect the cultural rules and expected behaviors. This is likely to happen in nearly every organization. If you wish to preserve your culture, the management team must step up and address the behavior with the individual and force a change, or failing that, the person will have to leave the company. It cannot be that the expectations of behavior are not applied consistently to everyone. No individual employee can be given a pass because he or she shows great results while causing significant collateral damage in the process.

We've all spent our fair share of time carefully crafting mission and vision statements, only to watch them gather dust on the shelves with little connection to the company they were designed to guide. If you want your operating principles to take hold, you must make sure that they become an integral part of your active, day-to-day organi-zational culture.[2]

If the creation of a proactive conscious culture seems too daunting for you and your senior team, you can get help from independent consultants who can help you through this process. Depending on the size and complexity of your organization, there might be some merit in hiring an expert to pull together the information neces-sary to make the decisions about changes in your company's culture. However, if you have a strong senior team who is well connected to the staff, it is usually possible to do this in-house. The important thing to remember is to be sure to connect the information inputs to the desired outputs so that the resulting culture is grounded in fact and administered through systems. Vague directives without practi-cal follow-through can create confusion and ineffective behavior.

Figure 10.2 shows what a completed profile of a conscious cultural initiative might look like.

Figure 10.2   Example of completed culture model

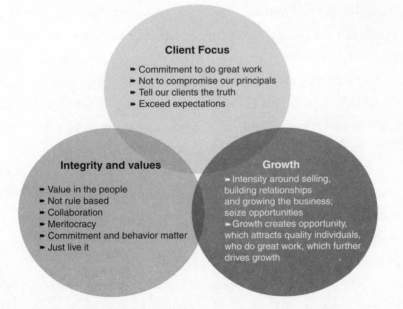

THE POWER OF CULTURE

Cultures are a lot like the personality of an organization; generally, they are not hard to find and hard to hide. Every business has its own culture. Some cultures are collaborative and supportive; others are more Darwinian and cutthroat, and still others are regimented and rule-focused. But no matter what the culture, it takes on a life of its own that influences everyone who interacts with the company both inside and outside.

During my time at GE, I learned a great deal about the power of corporate culture. Somewhat rigid, rule-based, and hierarchical, it was a culture that valued performance. Exceed your goals, follow a limited set of certain rules and guidelines, and you would be rewarded. There was little tolerance for not adhering to the GE way of executing your role and even less patience with not hitting performance targets.

To emphasize this operational principle, the company culture heavily focused on people development. Nearly all of the professional staff received formal training each and every year, and this training included both product or technical updates and skills training. The company invested in these programs to show you how to perform at peak levels. As a result, mediocre performance was not tolerated. This part of the culture was tough but dynamic and did produce results.

People development in ways other than just training was also part of the culture. Talented people were routinely identified through a formal and informal approach and were put on a path to new assignments and new "stretch roles" designed to push boundaries and spur growth.

GE had other cultural characteristics that I thought were quite positive and contributed to a growth culture as well. Debate and, sometimes, very heated discussion were encouraged. If you had a point of view, you were expected to make it known and stand your ground, even if your view wasn't a popular one.

So why is the culture at a place as big as GE relevant for a second-stage entrepreneur? Certainly, big companies do not do everything well, but there are valuable lessons one can learn by studying the cultures that lead these big companies to sustained success. By selectively assimilating specific aspects proven to work in these large companies, you will bolster your efforts to create your own company culture.

CREATING A CONSCIOUS CULTURE

My first start-up was at a firm called Alternative Resources Corporation (ARC). I was the number two executive, running all of field sales and operations, so naturally I had considerable impact on the culture. But the CEO was a great force as well, and one scheme he concocted had a dramatic impact on the conscious culture and on the ultimate success of the business.

ARC grew rapidly almost from its inception. Wind Point Partners, the private equity investor/owners, planned to either sell the company or perhaps undertake an initial public offering when the time was right. However, growth is expensive, and capital resources were tight.

As a result, when building the sales and operations teams, our primary recruitment strategy was to find young talented individuals who would work for affordable salaries. The average age in this hypergrowth company was well under 30. We sought out young people who perhaps did not have significant corporate experience but were highly talented, ambitious, and looking to build their career.

In the company's fourth year of operation, the CEO decided to introduce a game changer in terms of the company culture: a company-wide incentive. If we could hit a certain stretch revenue target for the company that year, everyone—and I mean everyone (and their spouse or significant other)—would be treated to a four-day company-paid trip to the Hyatt Regency in St. John, United States Virgin Islands.

This hard-target incentive had a powerful impact on the culture in rallying the people to work together to achieve a nearly impossible goal. It energized everyone from receptionist to the board room and created a powerful connection in the over thirty field offices in the United States and Canada that had not existed before.

The company made the revenue goal that year and everyone went on the trip. The benefits, both tangible and intangible, that came from this experience had a profound effect on the company culture. Many of the staff, especially those in lower level administrative or operational roles, became strongly committed to the company. Unplanned turnover at all levels went down to near zero, and the level of partnership between offices rose to an all-time high.

The collaboration and sense of shared mission helped to drive amazing growth. The success of the culture change due to the incentive was so dramatic that the CEO used it the following year and the results were equally stellar. All these years later, if you talk to individuals who were part of the company at that time, many will tell you they never worked so hard and never had as great an experience.

ARC had started from a business plan in 1988 with total capital of $2 million. By 1994, two years after the incentive culture change, it surpassed the $100 million revenue run rate. All of the growth was organic. We would open an office, staff the office with sales and operations personnel, train and support the local team, and the revenue from that office would begin to grow. That same year the company completed a highly successful public offering. In early1996, the company had a market capitalization of over $600 million.

When I left ARC at the end of 1994 to start Parson Group, I took the lessons on the benefit of building a strong culture, built on young, talented people and company-wide incentives. From the start, we frequently brought various teams together in high-quality locations, such as Telluride, Colorado, or Lake Owen, Wisconsin, two of the most beautiful places in the country. These meetings would alternate between management groups, sales, and operations. We made a specific point to include all roles within the company and we included all levels, since we felt that every role in the company contributed to the growth plan. The meetings reinforced the culture we were trying to build and connected the various teams to the operating strategy—and to their peers from around the country with equal parts of work and play. Holding a meeting of this type is a significant investment in dollars spent to transport, feed, and house a large group. There is also the cost of time not in the office driving the business. Nonetheless, we were convinced the time and money had a high return on investment.

Parson grew to become one of the fastest growing start-ups in the nation at the time, and was ranked as the number one fastest growing private company in the United States by *Inc. Magazine*. The culture we developed played a very important part in our success. As with ARC, if you ask employees who were part of that experience, they will tell you that they have not experienced anything quite like it since.

When you talk with Doug Zell of Intelligentsia coffee, he will tell you that it was only recently that his company began to have a conscious focus on the culture. A big part of the culture has always been the passion for the product and the commitment to make the very best coffee possible. Like Founders Brewing, Zell's company worried less about the cost of producing the product because it was convinced that based on quality, there would be considerable flexibility when setting the price. The culture of Intelligentsia began to change when the company opened its first store in Los Angeles. The success of the Los Angeles location did two things. It demonstrated the "ridiculous" volume that was possible from a single location. Second, this is when, dissatisfied with the quality of the beans they were able buy, the company started down the path of directly sourcing beans from growers around the world. Today, the commitment to quality is still the central underpinning of Intelligentsia's culture. Doug will point out that *quality* is the best position to defend. He believes that a focus on quality will fuel continued growth, and this emphasis on growth in now becoming a central part of the culture as well. The desire is to build a growing company so that this growth can create opportunities for the people who work there. There is also a shared passion for insuring that both the suppliers and customers do well. This is unusual today, as many companies aggressively try to manage their supplier's margins to a razor-thin level and for the most part treat their suppliers as vendors, not as partners. This practice is totally foreign to Intelligentsia. As an example of this commitment to its suppliers, Intelligentsia holds an annual meeting where its grower partners from around the world can get together to share best practices and compare notes. Similarly, part of the role of Intelligentsia's sales team is a kind of customer advocacy; the company wants its customers to be convinced that Intelligentsia really cares about their success—because in fact it really does care. My guess is that this is a big factor in a company's success. Doug would agree with this point overall. He believes that culture will eat strategy for breakfast and that a focus on quality and on your customers will allow you to persevere through the tough challenges along the way.

PARTING WORDS

Culture matters now more than ever. In these rapidly changing times, in your own rapidly evolving company, culture can be the rudder that guides your path to second-stage entrepreneurship in a fashion that is consistent with your vision and values.

As you step into second-stage entrepreneurship, it is critical to examine the culture that exists in your firm today and determine which aspects support your plan for the future and which need to be changed. Take a step back and work with your team to create a conscious culture. Implement and reinforce the values and operating principles with clear behaviors and guidelines to keep the culture healthy and thriving. Make sure your incentives and disincentives support the culture and behaviors you value. You will discover that a dynamic corporate culture will be the cornerstone to building your business.

Chapter 11

THE KEYS TO EFFECTIVE LEADERSHIP

WARREN BENNIS, THE LEGENDARY organization expert and pioneer of modern leadership principles, famously said, "Leadership is the capacity to translate a vision into reality." Taking this statement a bit further, we can characterize leadership as the quality that inspires people to do their best every day. Without effective leadership, any organization will flounder and get lost in a thicket of conflicting agendas and priorities. Without inspired leaders, an organization's mission, vision, values, and direction become unclear and growth suffers.

As a company enters second-stage growth, the need for effective leadership increases dramatically. The founder can no longer touch each person each day, and unlike in the early days when the entire team was in essence "family," the increasing size of the organization makes interacting with each person in a personal way far more difficult. When you then add in geographic and time zone considerations, this personal touch no longer can be a face-to-face daily interaction. The founder has to step it up and learn to both lead and manage differently than in the early days.

LEADERSHIP AND MANAGEMENT

Both leadership and management are equally necessary components for any successful company. In the best-case scenarios, each lends itself to improving the other as well as the organization as a whole. But there are critical and distinct differences that we should keep in mind as we move forward. Leadership is really about the big picture. It's about creating a vision for the organization, instilling a set of values throughout the culture of the organization that become its guiding principles, and making sure that everyone fully commits to them.

The discipline of management focuses on productivity, processes, and systems. Once the vision and goals are established for a business, the management team is responsible for the coordination of the nuts-and-bolts internal mechanisms for achieving success. The principal purpose of management is to create and sustain repeatable and even habitual systems that reduce variability in outcomes. If all systems are firing on all cylinders, effective management is essential if the company is to grow.

To take a second-stage example, consider the Novo Group, a Milwaukee-based company that focuses on delivering a much more effective approach to providing recruitment support for their corporate clients. Cindy Lu, the founder of the business, established the vision for this innovative approach to recruitment. It is based on effective and efficient management of the recruitment process by her staff for client companies. The overall recruitment process is broken down into discrete steps. Using supply chain principles, specific staff members conduct each discrete step in the overall process. The assignment of tasks to perform is based on staff member's skill set.

Because this cost-effective approach to recruitment is quite different from the way most firms handle this function, the Novo Group must rely on tight management of every step of the process to insure that its clients are well served and that the end product is delivered in a fashion that matches the overall value proposition.

In Novo's early days, with just one location, Cindy was able to manage her start-up company by just walking around the office and checking in with her staff. After its growth to second stage and expansion to locations in four different cities, Cindy's hands-on daily management process had to change. She evolved her primary skill from management to leadership. Now she has managers at each location to supervise the process while she guides their message to keep the vision of the company moving forward.

This natural evolution of skills is typical of most second-stage entrepreneurs. As their start-up grows in size and scope, they must learn to lead and delegate the daily management to a trusted senior team. The sales process is a perfect example. As we've seen, it is not a practical idea for the CEO to manage the sales team, especially when it is expanded into a larger organization servicing bigger geographic territories. The details of defined sales process and the myriad daily interventions necessary to coach and develop, troubleshoot problems and keep the salespeople on track and on message are time-consuming and too complex.

In any second-stage company, the founder has to step back and into a leadership role. He or she has to make sure everyone in the company understands what the company is all about, where it is going, how the company will get there, and the role that each employee plays in the realization of the vision. This is a leadership function vital to new and sustained growth.

Eddie Lou, the founder and CEO of Shiftgig has a very evolved perspective of leadership, which is unusual for the CEO in a technology company still in the very early stage. Perhaps his ten years in venture capital investing and serving on the boards of young companies taught him the importance of great leadership. First, a leader must be able to paint a vision—both inside and outside the company. The insiders include the management team and the rest of the employees. The outsiders include investors, the market, media, and others who are following the company. The leadership style at Shiftgig is to set "achievable but aggressive" metrics and rally the team to hit as many of the stretch targets as possible. Shiftgig leadership tries to walk the fine line between empowering employees and at the same time pursuing a sort of relentless search for potential areas of improvement in the company, the product, and the plans for growth. The approach resembles that of "trust, but verify" and is quite appropriate for a company at such an early stage.

While it is not advisable for the CEO or founder to also try to be the sales manager in a second-stage company, this does not mean that effective leadership does not encompass effective selling skills. Actually, selling is an integral part of leadership, even if a majority of CEOs have not received any formal training in selling effectively. For example, consider the fact that over one half of the students graduating from college throughout the United States each year end up in a role as a sales person. Despite this fact, says Howard Stevens, chairman of Chally, a global sales assessment provider, of the over 4,000 schools in the United States, only a few dozen offer a degree in sales or sales management. So, how many CEOs of second-stage companies are actually skilled in selling? I am not sure, but I know that if you were to ask the professional salespeople in each of those companies, they would tell you that the actual number is far less than the number of CEOs who think they are good at this skill.

Eddie Lou, founder and CEO of Shiftgig, believes that it is absolutely essential for all CEOs of second-stage growth companies to be able to sell effectively. In Eddie's view, first-rate sales skills are necessary to pitch your story to potential investors, to communicate with your technical team about why certain product features are necessary, and to convince potential employees that they should agree to be paid below-market salaries, but receive equity based on the theory that this will be a far better deal for them in the long run. Then, of course, nearly every second-stage CEO is in front of customers and prospects on a regular basis building relationships, and demonstrating knowledge of the industry, market, and potential competitors in a way that supports the sales strategy and selling efforts of the sales team

As discussed earlier, everyone is born with certain behavioral tendencies and personality traits that will determine his or her likely innate skill at selling. Some of the traits necessary to be really good at selling just cannot be taught. But like leadership training, sales training will raise your basic level of competency. Everyone, regardless of his or her basic personality, can get incrementally better at selling. Yes, it is true that perhaps you don't have to be the very best sales person in your company, but developing the skill to an acceptable level is quite important. Most CEOs sell every day. If you have not been trained in the science of selling, reading up on the subject, getting some formal training, learning how to be more effective at this critical skill will pay dividends and will help propel growth.

LEADERSHIP AT ALL LEVELS

Leadership can and does exist at any and all levels in an organization. The founder's leadership role is to keep the company moving forward and keep an eye on the big picture of the future. However, all employees, whether they are managers or dedicated workers, can take on leadership roles. For managers, leadership means a deep understanding of how their specific team contributes to the organization and inspiring their reports to be successful in making that contribution. A salesperson or in-house administrator leads by taking the initiative to perform his or her roles beyond expectations and serving as a model for others to do the same.

For example, in a technology company, a product developer can demonstrate leadership attributes by using his or her knowledge of the deficiencies of existing products in the marketplace and building and executing a product development path that exploits the gaps to create a compelling product. By seizing this opportunity and working to lead the team to success, a single developer can be a force for change and a leader in a company.

TOP-DOWN LEADERSHIP

Having leaders throughout the company supports the overall effort to drive second-stage growth. However, this does not diminish the need to have effective leadership at the very top. Effective leaders have a strong bias toward action. Taking constructive, well-planned action consistent with the vision and goals of the organization serves as a beacon and as a model for the other leaders in the company. Leading with confidence while at the same time being open to suggestions and responsive to changes makes a strong leader.

Credibility and trust are critical when it comes to the leadership role. Leaders inspire people to do their best and more. Leaders who do not back up their stated intentions with action will find that their organization will lose faith in their leadership and will falter. Their credibility in the eyes of the staff will suffer. Indecision, equivocation, and delay concerning serious company initiatives sap the momentum necessary for growth.

For example, I did some consulting for a private equity-backed company based in the Midwest; the company was in the advertising and publishing industry. In order to turbocharge growth, the board of directors decided to bring in a new CEO with a plan to change the business model for this traditional company to one that had greater emphasis on social media and technology. In the first week, the new CEO came in and gave an inspiring talk about the great opportunity in front of the company, the need to change the business model, and the need for everyone to work together to fulfill the new vision using existing resources as cash was tight. This part of his first week was great.

However, upon arriving that first week in the corporate offices, he decided the old CEO's office was not big enough and the furniture not nice enough. Instead he took over the boardroom and purchased new, quite expensive furniture. Further, and perhaps worse, he instructed that the payment for the furniture be put through in several parts because that would look better than one large check. In his new leadership role, he had to travel to meet clients and visit branch offices. Contrary to his stated policy to keep costs down, he traveled first class even if the flight was under an hour. Not surprisingly, within the first month, everyone in the company knew that he did not follow the same standards he set for others. Employees were expected to work harder to achieve the new vision of the company without additional compensation or resources while their leader spent lavishly on himself, and this created widespread cynicism, depressed morale, and materially affected performance. This particular CEO did not last even one year in the role before the board had no choice but to fire him. This is an extreme example, but we have all seen various less severe versions of this same leadership pattern. If the CEO expects the team to work hard, he or she must show the way. If money is tight, it should be tight for everyone. If treating everyone with dignity and respect is a core value, it has to be a behavior everyone adheres to, including the senior management team. Employees tend to be very observant and are generally quite smart, and they will pay attention in the long run not to what leaders say, but to what leaders do.

TAKING STOCK

Putting vision into action requires thinking about leadership a bit differently. Fundamentally, this requires the ability to look at a situation with complete objectivity and then being able to discern what is necessary for success based on careful and shrewd observation. An effective leader understands the gaps between the current state of the organization and the future goal and what it will take to close that gap and thrive going forward.

Effective leadership requires nearly constant reevaluation of the organization and of its goals and resources. There are a series of questions that I believe spur this reassessment if they are answered objectively:

1. What values and behaviors do we stand for and what are the gaps between those values and how we behave as a company today?

2. Are we prepared to make the changes necessary to achieve success?

3. What do we have in terms of talent and what do we need to address the current market?

4. Do we have the current capital and organizational capacity to capitalize on the opportunities and mitigate the risks?

This all sounds like a straightforward exercise. Many of these points we've discussed earlier. However, for the leader of a successful start-up, this process can be challenging. Initial success can be deceptive and breed complacency, even in a push to second-stage development. Lack of success can cause frustration and bullheadedness and can sometimes impair the ability to develop insights. Complete objectivity is difficult when you were the one that assembled the team you are leading. Systems that have proven effective are difficult to change. Mistakes can be wrongly attributed to outside factors rather than to the organization itself. Jack Welch famously said, "Face reality as it is, not as it was or as you wish it to be." Effective leaders remain vigilant and must look beyond the distractions of the present to keep their organization focused on the goal of new growth and higher profitability. I would encourage you to ask the questions above with some frequency because in second-stage companies things can change rapidly. I would also encourage you to look for evidence supporting each of your answers; in effect, look for examples and data that cause you to answer the questions based on facts. I'd also suggest asking both your board and your employees these questions, though perhaps not phrased the same way. The answers may surprise you.

Maybe Andy Grove, former chairman and CEO of Intel, captured this notion best when he said, "Only the paranoid survive." His point is well taken though. One should never get complacent or overly confident, as a certain level of professional skepticism coupled with a relentless desire to always improve can serve the second-stage leader well.

QUALITIES OF STRONG LEADERSHIP

How can a leader guard against these obstacles to leadership? Over the years of working with leaders at all levels of businesses large and small, I found the following few concepts can make a big difference when striving for excellence in leadership. There is a large body of books and articles on this important topic, and I would encourage all of you to read those.

HAVE A HEALTHY EGO

Certainly no one gets to a leadership position without a strong ego. Self-confidence is a key component of leadership. But being able to balance ego with an openness to listen to ideas is the mark of a true leader. True leaders understand their strengths, and they will be well aware of their weaknesses and blind spots and able to move past them.

When leaders have a healthy ego, this means they have a balanced sense of their own importance, and their own strengths and weaknesses. More than any other personality weakness or management mistake, the lack of a healthy ego in a leader tends to derail even the best-laid plans for future growth in a company. Bluster, bullying, and rigidity of focus will alienate people and inspire fear, not respect. Weak, conflicted approaches to hard challenges, such as staff terminations, budget tightening, or contract negotiations create confusion and indecision. The ability to delegate authority, openness to change, willingness to admit mistakes and praise top performance in others, and most of all, consistency in policy decisions are the marks of a healthy, balanced ego in a leader. One of the key characteristics of effective leaders is their ability to learn from their mistakes. For example, Netflix fumbled in a major way in mid-2011 with an ill-conceived and poorly communicated pricing change for its streaming and DVD-by-mail services. After a customer revolt and the subsequent drop in the company's stock price, Reed Hasting, CEO and cofounder, apologized and, more important, implemented corrective action. In early 2013, Netflix reported its biggest quarterly growth spurt in new subscribers for streaming services in nearly three years—and its stock price rose by 35 percent in one day.

BALANCE POPULARITY AND EFFECTIVENESS

While popularity is not part of the job description, it can be a significant factor in effective leadership. Leaders who are universally disliked and feared cannot hope to motivate their organization. More likely, the best people will quit. Second-stage growth in particular requires putting in extra work and taking initiatives above and beyond the usual work cycle. This kind of commitment requires approachable, supportive leadership. That doesn't mean your colleagues should be your best friends. Far from it. But for leaders to be effective it is important to project and promote a culture of collegiality to make sure the job gets done.

Effective leadership requires the ability to not be afraid to be candid with your team. Sometimes the message is negative and requires actions that might be unpleasant such as trimming a budget, shutting down an important development project, or terminating personnel. The ability to deliver a difficult message, make sure it is heard, and still retain the respect of the team and a reputation as a fair and balanced manager is critical. Effective leaders need to couch communications with their staff, whether good news or bad, in a positive, constructive context. Praise peak performance publicly. Share good news about company success. By creating an overall persona of a supportive, appreciative leader, you will be able to gain the staff's acceptance of any challenges more easily.

This balanced approach can be a difficult thing for many second-stage entrepreneurs. By nature, they are aggressive and driven, focused on the goal of success. Tolerance is not their strong suit. They tend to believe they are always right. Many have historically operated based on the principle of "get on board or get out of the way," and their belief is that this attitude and approach has helped immeasurably in making them successful. They are seldom satisfied, even when great success is evident. There are some positive aspects to this personality type; however, as the business grows, this overall attitude and approach can have significant negative repercussions. Founders need to learn to appreciate the hard work of others and accept their role as leaders of both the charge ahead and the cheer for making each touchdown.

RESPOND TO CHANGE

Most revenue graphs are not charts that run straight north, nor are most business journeys conducted in a straight line. Some plans, products, and strategies work well, and some do not. Some work well for a period of time, and then things change and the past practice is, for some reason, no longer effective. It is critical for a leader to step back at regular intervals to assess progress against the existing plan and modify the plan if necessary.

Effective leaders are always on the lookout for ways to make their plans more relevant and up-to-date, their products and services more compelling, and their organization better overall.

Most second-stage companies do not have the resources to hire management consultants who can provide streams of market data and competitive intelligence to inform decisions and suggest where a change of plan would be timely. Instead, the leaders of those companies must learn to make decisions even when obtaining sufficient facts and data to get to certainty in the choice is not possible. Second-stage entrepreneurs must find alternative approaches to keep abreast of changing market conditions and varying degrees of effectiveness in the execution of the company's plan.

A number of years ago, I had a board member tell me the following story. "The first fall down a flight of stairs is a given. The second fall down that same flight of stairs is annoying, but I can understand how that happens. However, I find the third fall down that very same flight of stairs inexcusable." Inasmuch as this story was told to me as a result of some miscues that I had made, this has become a story I remember to this day for its emphasis on the need to learn from our mistakes.

Over the past two decades, there has been quite a bit of thought leadership on the subject of "paradigm shifts" and "disruption" that has occurred to products, services, and business models. Leaders across all industries became aware of the necessity to change, modify, or in some way transform their way of doing business in response to basic game changes in traditional models of finance, management style, and society. Today, especially in technology companies, the term "paradigm shifts" has been replaced by "pivot points."

Certain innovations and trends—whether technological, societal, economic, or political—can significantly impact the business environment. We do not have to look very far to see the wreckage of what were once large companies whose business model was completely disrupted as a result of some change in technology or a new regulation. No doubt, there were many more much smaller companies that were hit by these same changes, but we just don't hear as much about them because of their size. Effective leaders, always focused on the greater world outside their organizations, recognize these pivot points, and they respond to meet the new challenges (and opportunities) they create. Second-stage entrepreneurial leaders need to remain nimble and leverage the pivot points that resonate with their business to ride the wave to growth.

A number of the companies we have discussed throughout this book have gone through a time when they realized that they could change a product and their market approach or seize a larger market opportunity if they just changed a few things or organized in some different way. In some cases, more than a few things had to change.

Founders Brewing had this epiphany six years ago when Dave Engbers and Mike Stevens staved off bankruptcy, moved into a new location, changed the entire product line from making "unremarkable" beer and instead committed to making great beer. This change has propelled the company to become the fastest growing brewery in the world. Bob Sanders of AXIOM SFD recognized that the historical way of training salespeople was outdated. He came back to the company where he had once been a partner and embarked on a major project to change the way sales training is delivered. He went out and raised the capital necessary to fund this change. Gene Zaino of MBO Partners recognized that while being focused on providing a turnkey approach for supporting independent contractors in growing and managing their business was working well, there was a potentially lucrative opportunity available to build an entirely new line of business by establishing a targeted effort at the large companies employing significant numbers of independent contractors. He hired a new executive to create and execute the plan to build this business. Paying attention to pivot points can be rewarding.

BE PRESENT AND VISIBLE

Second-stage entrepreneurship can be all-consuming. While changing your company, chasing capital, hiring your team, and focusing on growth, you are also transforming many aspects of your role as hands-on founder. As you expand, there are new demands on your time. Meetings with board members. Meetings with off-site managers. Meeting with clients, vendors, investors. Your attention to these various groups is critical if you are to lead effectively.

However, it is easy to get distracted. Mobile technology is relentless. Messages, emails, and text messages bombard us all the time, and we often interrupt what we're doing with the familiar phrase: "Can you give me a minute please. I really have to get this call." Not only does this break your concentration on the meeting or issue at hand, it can be insulting to the person who has only a few precious moments of your time. Almost as bad is a tendency to respond to emails or text messages while you are supposed to be meeting with someone.

Another distraction is the perception of your role as leader, not a manager. Ever since you started the company, you've had to wear so many hats: manager, creator, salesperson, accountant, marketer, even mailroom clerk. In the early days at Founders Brewing, for example, Mike and Dave did everything including working the bar, brewing the beer, ordering supplies, and making sales calls. It's difficult to just turn off the urge to be hands-on when you see something that needs to be done or fixed. In the old days, you would take the time to do it yourself, or direct someone to take care of the problem if you had employees. However, as a second-stage leader, you really can't afford the time anymore, so it is important to resist the urge to continue old behaviors and do things yourself rather than letting one of the managers do their job and deal with the issue.

As the company leader, you need to guard against being distracted. While time management gurus hail multitasking as the most efficient use of time, this doesn't hold true for top leaders. People expect and need you to focus on whatever meeting or conversation you take the time to engage in. Taking calls, answering messages, and worrying about minor details dilute your ability to devote your full attention, to make meaningful comments, to in fact *be present*.

This simple tenet applies to leaders, no matter what the size or stage of their company. There is one CEO I know well who runs a $10 billion global company. You will not get very much of his time, but when you do, he will be totally focused on the discussion for the entire time that you are with him. He will have read and digested any materials you sent him in advance and will be prepared to discuss the topic in detail while you meet. Ironically, in many smaller companies, it is less likely that the CEO will display this kind of focus. Second-stage entrepreneurs are particularly prone to distraction.

As a corollary to this idea, effective leaders must be visible to their staff. Don't make the mistake of holing up in your office and taking meetings only with senior managers. This creates the impression that you are unapproachable and have outgrown the connection you once had with the people who work for you. It is important to budget time to visit with the departments, walk around the facility, visit branch offices on a rotating basis, be *physically present*. Just as it is important for clients to put a face to the company name, it is equally important for the employees to see that you're around and to know who you are. This is another part of *being present*.

KNOW YOUR LIMITS

In a rapidly growing company, understanding your own level of competence as a leader is not simple. In the beginning, everyone came to you for answers. Sometimes you had answers; sometimes you winged it with varying results. However, as a second-stage entrepreneur, you've got more at stake. False steps impede growth. While I am not suggesting you abandon intuition, decisions generally must be based on data and planning. As the leader, you need to rely on the strong team you assembled to provide information to fill in the gaps in your own knowledge.

Know your limits, acknowledge them, and seek help when needed so you can lead effectively. Asking questions doesn't cost anything. Make uninformed or ego-driven decisions often does.

PARTING WORDS

Effective leadership becomes increasingly important as the company grows into the second stage. As the founder, you can no longer keep track of everything that is necessary to execute your plan, and you are forced to rely on your team. Management skills still matter, but leadership becomes more important. You have to get things done through others. Having the leadership presence and skill helps your entire company buy into the vision and culture of your organization.

Good leadership is one of those skills that we can all get better at. There are some innate qualities that leaders are born with, but we can all learn much of what we need to know to be effective. Better leaders, just as they always question and challenge the company's plan, constantly seek to understand how well they are performing as leaders and how they can improve. Becoming a better leader will help you have a profound impact on your company's overall results and will inspire your team to do the best possible job every day.

Appendix

EXIT STRATEGY: MOVING ON

A NUMBER OF YEARS AGO, WHILE RUNNING Parson Group, one of the outside directors, a talented executive and true gentleman by the name of Don Perkins, talked to me about his views on the subject of CEO succession, which in the corporate world in many ways is equivalent to an exit strategy.

Perkins felt that at some point—which he defined as around ten years or so—nearly every CEO will better serve the organization that he or she is running by deciding to "move on." I think at the time I had been running Parson Group for six years. Funny, after listening to Don, I thought to myself, "I am just getting started on this venture." Further, I was still in my early forties at the time.

While this notion of "ten years" may seem too brief a period for some and quite a stretch for others, you'll welcome his viewpoint when you realize that Don had a very interesting perspective and history that helped him come to this unique point of view.

Don had come out of Harvard Business School and gone right to Jewel Foods, which was at the time a midsize grocery store chain based in Chicago. Don rose rapidly in the ranks at Jewel, and he became CEO at the age of 45. At the age of 55, after serving as CEO for ten years, a period during which Jewel enjoyed dramatic growth, he shocked nearly everyone in the organization by "retiring."

Unlike Don, who viewed his exit as part of the natural process of his leadership cycle, many CEOs see their exit as a form of failure and postpone the inevitable far beyond the point when their leadership is no longer the best thing for the company.

One trait of a generous exit strategy is remembering that it's not all about you. While we all want to go out on top and while we can still enjoy doing what we love most, we must also consider what we leave behind and those who will remain after we're gone. So part and parcel of moving forward is looking back, reflecting on where you've been and how to move forward so that to the extent this is possible, it's a win-win for everyone involved.

The theory is that at some point in time nearly all of us lose the ability to be as passionate, committed, and objective as we were when we started our tenure as company leader. Most executives will tell you this is true in the corporate world, and it is what I have seen in scores of smaller successful start-ups that grew to a scale. Entrepreneurs who have worked hard to build their companies and achieved their milestone of wealth and success often cash out and go on to start other businesses that interest them.

According to the Exit Planning Institute, over 50 percent of the owners of privately held businesses say they expect to have a change in ownership within the next 15 years. As a result of this, these business owners are expected to generate $10 trillion in personal liquidity over the same period of time through the sale of these businesses. The research also suggests that very few actually plan for an exit, a situation the Institute is attempting to remedy.

Planning your exit strategy from the company you started and made successful is complex and emotional. Each company and its founder have their own set of factors that result in the decision to exit. As a general rule, founders who have a controlling interest in their business do not look for an exit unless there is some significant trigger event. This could be age, estate planning, health, or a desire to relocate. If a founder took in capital to pursue a second-stage growth strategy, there is usually some language in the financing agreement that will designate some kind of timetable or condition. Investors, particularly private equity investors, target companies with the idea that they will be sold when market conditions are optimal.

Regardless of your financial arrangements in the company, it pays to have some kind of exit strategy in place, even if it is still years before the actual event.

QUIT WHILE YOU'RE AHEAD

I think that you will agree that the absolute best time to exit a business or to turn over the helm to your successor is when the company has a consistent track record of growth in both revenue and profits, and you can credibly make the case that the growth is likely to continue—even if the leadership will be different in the future. In the case of selling the business, the less drama, resentment, or disruption that accompanies your plan to leave the company, the more positively that will reflect on any potential sale. In many cases, the buyer of the company will view the fact that the founder is moving on as a positive sign of future transition. Even private equity buyers who have no desire to actually run the company commonly want to install a different CEO or even a different top team to run the company after a transaction closes.

However, it is not always feasible to exit a company at its peak. Despite your best efforts to lead the company forward, if there are serious issues with the company that any buyer can see, such as flat or declining revenue, client concentration, legal battles, or challenges with profitability, the buyer will be in a position of leverage for significant discounts on the purchase price due to these deficiencies. The decision to exit under these circumstances gets more complicated.

BEGINNING THE PLANNING PROCESS

The question concerning your exit strategy doesn't involve artificial time limits or wealth goals. It is simple and straightforward: when is the right time for *you*? While this decision is unique to each founder, there are some general issues that are part of planning an exit strategy. Below is a list of questions that you might ask to help guide you in your decision on when a sale of the business or a transfer of the role to your successor. You might ask the following questions to begin thinking about structuring your own exit strategy:

- What were your original goals in forming the company and have you achieved them to your own satisfaction?
- Have changes in the marketplace presented challenges that you might not be willing to address at this stage?
- Are the legacy issues concerning the company also impacting family and siblings?
- How will your lifestyle change if you exit from the company?
- Do you have plans to start other projects or companies after your exit?
- How will your exit affect your colleagues and staff?
- How will it affect the future of the company?
- What is your financial stake in the company and how will you benefit from exiting?
- How is an exit strategy affected by your arrangement with creditors and/or investors?

Of course, there are no correct answers to any these questions, only answers that are right for you and your company.

LATE-STAGE ENGAGEMENT

When evaluating the performance of a team member, one of the critical points is whether he or she is working at peak performance, devoting 100 percent to the company. If you apply this criterion to yourself as the CEO of the company, how will you fare? As the leader of the organization, if you are not firing on all pistons, all the time, your team will notice it, and employees will begin to question both the organization's future as well as their own. Chances are if your people notice your lack of engagement, others outside the company will also notice it. Remember, it's not just you that you have to consider, but the health of the organization under your command as well as its potential sale to outsiders who are just as savvy as you.

It does seem hard to imagine that a founder would ever be less than 100 percent committed. After all, founders typically own the controlling interest in the company, and it is likely that most of their net worth is tied up in the value of the business. But this is much more common than you think, especially in multigenerational family businesses and businesses that are generating substantial cash. The likelihood of this happening is significantly less in a second-stage company, as executing the plan to drive rapid growth is all consuming and tends to energize the entire team.

Because of your leadership role, others carefully observe you in almost everything you do. Small things that, perhaps, are not done are never missed, and everything that is done is magnified due to the role. If you're mentally not 100 percent in the game, your company will know it, and if you've physically altered your routine, no longer keeping regular hours or showing up for morning meetings, you are sending a bigger signal than you know.

In business, as in sports and in life in general, the difference between different outcomes—the difference between winning and not winning—is often due to very small actions and, in some cases, seemingly unimportant small things. For example, the difference between the number one ranked golfer in the world and the worst player on the PGA tour is typically less than three strokes per round over the course of a season. These "micromatters" either happen or they don't during the life of the business—or in the pursuit of a given sale—just as they happen or don't happen as part of the sale process.

Just as a key game between two equally capable opponents is typically won or lost because of a couple of key plays or a pass that is made or missed, businesses thrive because of a commitment to perform as well as possible each and every day. That commitment flows from the top down and will last as long as you help it thrive throughout the company. We've all been there. Burnout can be a bigger problem at the top than anywhere else, and due to our executive position, we feel not only that we're justified in taking some time off—even if it's only "mental"—but that no one should notice and, if they do, no one should complain anyway. That is why going out while on top is such a critical factor; anything less puts the company at risk to deal with a rough transition to the next CEO or, even worse, with a "fire sale" that won't nearly maximize the company's value as much as if you had left while you were at the top of your game.

And if you no longer have it in you to be 100 percent committed each and every day, particularly when everyone else in the organization is, it might be time to consider your exit strategy. I have seen many founders delay their exit despite this lack of commitment, primarily because based on the current performance of the business, they cannot achieve the valuation they somehow think is correct. So they delay, thinking that perhaps another year or maybe two will be enough to fundamentally change the performance track the company is on. This is possible, but it is more likely that based on the founder's commitment level, the company performance does not improve and may even get worse.

THE OUT OF SYNC SYNDROME

When CEOs overstay their welcome or stay past their expiration date, performance is one of the first things to suffer simply because, day by day, the CEO's lack of enthusiasm and less than 100 percent commitment filters down to the rest of the organization until at last everyone seems to be standing in place or, worse, slipping slightly backward. It is in some ways the same point made in chapter 1 that suggests if you are not growing, you are dying. Straddling the line, or treading water, is very difficult to do while keeping the company in sync. It is a strategy that repeatedly fails.

The issue of performance is a slightly tricky question for many CEOs, as it is typically very difficult to try to exit a business (or particularly to sell it) when things are *not* going so well. On the other hand, if the business is underperforming its peer group, then there must be a plan to once again improve prospects for growth in revenue and profit. If a business is losing ground to competitors, this is a very serious issue.

The important thing to remember when discussing performance, particularly your own, is to have an open mind. You've come this far with the company, and to go out gracefully you will need to look at yourself objectively and determine whether or not you still have some gas left in the tank or whether it's time to pull over and let someone else take the wheel.

A good board can play an invaluable role here. Unlike the management team and the CEO, who tend to be fully engaged in the day-to-day operations and deep in the "out of sync" mode I talked about earlier, a board or an individual board member can offer the objective input to you need to make your decision to potentially exit the company.

THE OUTSIDE VIEW

You should not only look inside the company for signs that it may be the right time to depart, but outside as well. There comes a time when external events can conspire to suggest that a changing of the guard is an advisable path. There are a variety of reasons that this might happen, and few of them have anything to do with you personally. It could be because market conditions have changed, for instance, or perhaps technological change has forced a modification in strategy.

Many times these external forces are accelerated and time-sensitive, making it harder for founders at the end of their tenure to find the intensity and motivation required to roll up their sleeves, redouble their efforts, and confront the new challenges head on; however, someone just taking over the reins might be better suited to the challenges.

Perhaps, for example, a product or service has become much more dependent on technology than you or your company anticipated. Or, based on market conditions, maybe the largest markets for a product or service have gone from primarily in the United States to mostly outside the United States. Perhaps the business has gone from hypergrowth to a path of slower growth because the field has become crowded with new competitors.

One of my clients, a successful second-stage manufacturer of outdoor products, became concerned about his market because of the surge of private equity money flooding the industry. His competitors were suddenly armed with more capital, new management teams, and snappy marketing plans. My client's firm was growing rapidly as a result of a number of successful new product releases, but the emergence of private equity-backed entrants into the market resulted in more risk in the operating environment for his company.

Should he stay the course and compete against these revamped businesses, or should he consider selling his company to a private equity firm that was making overtures to buy his firm? A "stay and invest" strategy likely would require taking his profit to zero in order to recruit new talent to compete with the new market entrants while at the same time changing the business model of the firm. Alternatively, he could sell the business at a substantial profit and move on. At this writing it is unclear what path this founder will choose. He is realistic about his chances to successfully transform his business, so he is implementing the organizational and business strategy that he believes necessary to grow the business, and at the same time he is beginning conversations with investment banks to see if there might be a buyer able to provide additional capital and fund the investment in the management talent that can take the business to the next level.

When these types of sea changes happen, sometimes a different executive with a different set of skills, more capital, or simply more energy or motivation because he or she is at the beginning of his or her tenure may be better equipped to lead the company at this juncture.

THE SUCCESSION QUESTION

A survey conducted by the National Association of Corporate Directors (NACD) found that only half of all companies surveyed—typically large companies—have a formal succession plan. The track record is even worse with smaller companies in which the founder serves as the CEO. A smooth leadership transition plan must be a significant factor in all exit strategies. Potential buyers often view the succession plan as an asset to the future of the company. It is important to your senior team and the other members of the company to know that a leader will be in place to keep the organization strong and growing.

If a succession plan is a critical piece to the future of any company, why is the track record regarding installing one so dismal at companies large and small? In part, this is human nature. It's a tough decision to plan a personal exit strategy. Planning for a successor to take your place is often even harder. Many leaders have made powerful contributions to their companies and find it difficult to think about someone stepping into that role and another person potentially changing or even undoing some of what they have built over years of tenure.

However, if you are considering moving on, you might consider surveying the playing field for your successor; it could make the exit process more real to you. Scouting, even mentoring, your successor could even mitigate the difficulties of departure phase because you would know that the company you've built, grown, and nurtured will now be in good hands.

SELLING AS AN EXIT STRATEGY

If you have outside investors, unless they are getting distributions, they will likely be applying pressure at some point that the business should be sold. After all, this is typically part of the up-front arrangement most professional investors make when providing financing for growth. While there may not be a fixed timetable for recouping their investment through the sale of the company, it is certainly a significant part of their plan for the future. In fact, most venture capital and private equity firms have an exit schedule that ranges from five to ten years, depending on the situation. Investors with a huge capital fund will expect to sell at the shorter end of the range; investors who provided capital to grow the company, not acquire it, tend to take a longer-term view.

When the market conditions are right—that is, when the opportunity arrives to sell the business at close to a premium price—the senior team will begin to feel the pressure from the investors to sell. Often the discussion will revolve around to the question of what the return on investment today looks like versus the risk and time-adjusted return on the investment if we wait another year or more. A significant factor is whether more investment will be necessary to increase the investors' overall ROI from a future sale. Whatever the time frame for the eventual sale, you'll need to start planning your exit strategy.

GREENER PASTURES

What holds many leaders back from seriously considering an exit strategy is the fear that their exit is the end of their business career. After spending decades building a business in a specific industry, it is hard to imagine much else once you leave it. But most leaders are driven people who live to meet challenges head-on. After a short time, in many cases even before they leave the company, they find opportunities that they can become energized about, inspired by, and committed to. It could be that they start or buy another company, join several boards of directors, or even enter the world of nonprofits. Exiting a company, even one you created, can be a new beginning. You'll have the time, talent, and most likely the capital to create an impact in whatever arena you choose.

PARTING WORDS

Leaving the company you started and built is never easy. No matter how profitable or timely your decision for leaving is, it really is like leaving home. Building a company is a time-intensive and emotional experience that also makes great demands on you personally, and you can never undo the amount of energy and experiences you've shared with a specific group of people in this most singular of endeavors.

Forming a specific and realistic exit strategy is important not just for its impact on you, but particularly for the second-stage entrepreneur, it matters because of how it affects those who've been a significant part of your journey. After all, without your team, success would not have been possible. It is important to start planning as early as possible. Evaluate your options. Search out a successor. Make the final transition as smooth as possible in order to leave your team and your company at the right time, in the right way, and in the right hands.

NOTES

INTRODUCTION

1. Edward Lowe Foundation, 2nd Stage Growth Companies, 2013, http://edwardlowe.org/who-we-serve/secondstage/.
2. Nicole Perlroth, "Technology Start Up Investors Grow Wary of Tech Ventures," The *New York Times*, January 13, 2013, Wahttp://www.nytimes.com/2013/01/14/technology/start-up-investors-grow-wary-of-tech-ventures-after-facebooks-ipo.html?pagewanted=all.

1 GROW OR DIE

1. Garret Ellison, "Why Some Say Founders Brewing Represents the Best of New Grand Rapids, Grand Rapids Press, November 16, 2012, http://www.mlive.com/business/west-michigan/index.ssf/2012/11/founders_impact_grand_rapids.html.
2. Garret Ellison, "How Flirting with Bankruptcy Forged @FoundersBrewing into a Titan of Craft Beer," Grand Rapids Press, October 5, 2012, http://www.mlive.com/business/west-michigan/index.ssf/2012/10/founders_15-year_anniversary.html.
3. Lueders Consulting website as source for volume statistics, http://www.brewconsult.com.

2 NEW CAPITAL SOURCES

1. Samuel Lee and Petra Persson, "Financing from Family and Friends," New York University Working Paper, March, 2012.
2. Startupnation.com, "Financing Options for a Small Business, Finding the Right Funding," http://www.startupnation.com/business-articles/890/1/AT_FindingFundingThatsRight.asp.

3. Data from National Venture Capital Association Report, http://www
.nvca.org/index.php?option=com_content&view=article&id=344&
Itemid=103.
4. Data are from the annual Bain & Co. Annual Report on Private Equity,
http://www.bain.com/bainweb/publications/global_private_equity_report
.asp.
5. Data from a 2012 Robert W. Baird & Co. proprietary report.
6. Garret Ellison, "Founders Brewing Plans Taproom Expansion," Grand Rapids
Press, February 27, 2013, http://www.mlive.com/business/west-michigan
/index.ssf/2013/02/founders_taproom_expansion.html.

4 CREATE, DON'T COMPETE

1. Data and history from Whole Foods website: http://www.wholefoods
market.com/company-info/whole-foods-market-history.
2. Sam Sifton, "Now Appearing in Chicago, A Restaurant in Footlights," The
New York Times, August 16, 2011 http://www.nytimes.com/2011/08/17
/dining/reviews/rstaurant-review-next-in-chicago.html?pagewanted=all.
3. "Alinea Named Top US Restaurant," "http://www.huffingtonpost.com/2010
/04/26/alinea-top-us-restaurant_n_552379.html" \1 "s84971title=1_Noma
_in".
4. Themes and prices from Alinea website, https://content.alinearestaurant
.com/html/index.html.
5. Alex Morris, "The Carefully Cultivated Soul of SoulCycle," New York
Magazine, January 2013.
6. Danielle Braff, "New Spin on Working Out," Chicago Tribune, September
26, 2012.
7. The SoulCycle Corporate website, www.soul-cycle.com.
8. Wellness Wire, "Equinox Buys SoulCycle and Plans Major Expansion,"
May 25, 2011 www.wellandgoodnyc.com.

5 HIRING SMART!

1. James Collins, Good to Great: Why Some Companies Make the Leap and others Don't, HarperBusiness, 2001.
2. Peter Cappelli, The New Deal at Work: Managing the Market-Driven Work-
force, Harvard Business School Press, 1999.
3. Matthew Dixon and Brent Adamson, The Challenger Sale: Taking Control of
the Customer Conversation, Portfolio Books, 2011.

4. Bernard Girard, *The Google Way: How One Company Is Revolutionizing Management as We Know It*, No Starch Press, 2009.

6   THE NEW MODEL FOR SELLING

1. Data on WebFilings assembled from company website, searches on social media, and conversations/correspondence with company employees, some posted on social media.
2. Information on Brandtrust assembled from company website and interview with the CEO.
3. Matthew Dixon and Brent Adamson, *The Challenger Sale: Taking Control of the Customer Conversation*, Portfolio Books, 2011.
4. For a much more detailed explanation of the concept of a trusted advisor, I would suggest a the reader consult the book: David Maister, Charles Green, and Robert Galford, *The Trusted Advisor*, Touchstone, 2001.
5. For a different, but very valuable read on the power of stories, I suggest the book written by Craig Wortmann, *What's Your Story, Using Stories to Ignite Performance and Be More Successful*, Kaplan Publishing, 2006.
6. Mahan Kalsa and Randy Illig, *Let's Get Real or Let's Not Play: Transforming the Buyer*, Portfolio Hardcover, 2008.

7   MANAGING BEYOND METRICS

1. CSO Insights, 2011 and 2012 Sales Management Optimization Studies, http://www.csoinsights.com/Publications.
2. Research from Chally website, www.chally.com.
3. Matthew Dixon and Brent Adamson, *The Challenger Sale: Taking Control of the Customer Conversation*, Portfolio Books, 2011.

8   GROWTH MARKETING

1. Manpower International website, http://www.manpower.com.

9   THE TOTAL CUSTOMER EXPERIENCE

1. Jeoffrey Bean and Sean Van Tyne, *The Customer Experience Revolution: How Companies like Apple, Amazon and Starbucks Have Changed Business Forever*, Brigantine Media, 2012.

2. James Heskett, Earl Sasser, and Leonard Schlesinger, *The Service-Profit Chain*, The Free Press, 1997.

10   CULTURE MATTERS

1. Entrepreneur Magazine website, "Corporate Culture," http://www.entrepre neur.com/encyclopedia/corporate-culture.
2. Lominger, now part of Korn-Ferry International, furnished the tools and process used by the internal consultants at Capital H Group as a guide for developing a conscious culture. http://www.lominger.com.

INDEX